DESIGNING INSTRUCTION
FOR
ADULT LEARNERS

Second Edition

The Professional Practices in Adult Education and Human Resource Development Series explores issues and concerns of practitioners who work in the broad range of settings in adult and continuing education and human resource development.

The books are intended to provide information and strategies on how to make practice more effective for professionals and those they serve. They are written from a practical viewpoint and provide a forum for instructors, administrators, policy makers, counselors, trainers, managers, program and organizational developers, instructional designers, and other related professionals.

Michael W. Galbraith
Editor-in-Chief

DESIGNING INSTRUCTION FOR ADULT LEARNERS

Second Edition

Gary J. Dean

KRIEGER PUBLISHING COMPANY
MALABAR, FLORIDA
2002

Original Edition 1994
Second Edition 2002

Printed and Published by
KRIEGER PUBLISHING COMPANY
KRIEGER DRIVE
MALABAR, FLORIDA 32950

FROM A DECLARATION OF PRINCIPLES JOINTLY ADOPTED BY A COM-
MITTEE OF THE AMERICAN BAR ASSOCIATION AND A COMMITTEE OF
PUBLISHERS:

This publication is designed to provide accurate and authoritative information in
regard to the subject matter covered. It is sold with the understanding that the
publisher is not engaged in rendering legal, accounting, or other professional service.
If legal advice or other expert assistance is required, the services of a competent
professional person should be sought.

Library of Congress Cataloging-in-Publication Data

Dean, Gary J.
    Designing instruction for adult learners / Gary J. Dean. — 2nd ed.
        p.   cm. — (Professional practices in adult education and human
    resource development series)
    Includes bibliographical references and index.
    ISBN 1-57524-205-2 (alk. paper)
    1. Adult education—Curricula—Planning. 2. Instructional systems—
Design. I. Title. II. Series.

    LC5219 .D39 2002
    374′.01—dc21   2001038329

10   9   8   7   6   5   4   3   2

This work is dedicated
with love and respect to
Sandra Kay Flannery Dean

CONTENTS

PREFACE TO
THE SECOND EDITION

In this second edition of *Designing Instruction for Adult Learners*, the basic structure and content of the original edition have been maintained. Changes have been made to clarify language and some points made in the text. In addition, many of the exhibits, figures, and activities have been revised and updated. References have also been updated to reflect recent works and changes in the literature. The book remains a model to apply instructional design principles to a wide variety of adult education settings. The primary focus of this book is the application of instructional design to the development of classroom learning for adults.

The needs of adult educators for planning instruction are many and varied. First, there are a great many settings in which adult education occurs—vocational schools, colleges and universities, religious institutions, the military, and correctional institutions, to name just a few. Second, there are a great many subjects studied in adult education—basic skills, vocational skills, liberal arts and humanities, personal enrichment, recreation, professional development, health, and may others. Third, adults engage in learning for may different reasons—some are personal fulfillment, career advancement, escape, and to help others. Fourth, there are many levels of adult educators in the field, from untrained volunteers to professionals with doctorates.

Among this variety of purpose and position, there are two common activities of adult educators: planning and facilitating

effective instruction. May resources in adult education are devoted to helping adult educators become better facilitators of
adult learning; this book addresses the planning process—what
adult educators do before they meet their learners.

The approach advocated in this book is the application of
instructional design to adult education, a systematic process by
which decisions are made about developing learning activities.
The basic process of instructional design consists of identifying
learning goals and objectives, developing learning activities to
meet those goals and objectives, and designing evaluation procedures to ensure that the goals and objectives have been met.
The approach advocated here has a new twist—the instructional
design process has been adapted to meet the needs of adult educators. This instructional design model is a comprehensive planning process which possesses a combination of structure and
flexibility, and therefore, can be used in numerous educational
settings, with a variety of topics and learners, and by all levels
of adult educators.

Three major topics are addressed in the book: gathering
information, developing the instructional plan, and evaluating
the instructional plan. In addition, an initial chapter presents an
overview of the model and addresses concerns about the use of
instructional design in adult education.

The first topic, gathering information, comprises Chapters
2 through 6. In these chapters, gathering information about
yourself as an adult educator, about content, learners, and learning contexts is described. Chapter 2 deals with assessing and
developing your skills as an adult educator and includes a review
of the literature regarding the behavior, beliefs, knowledge, and
skills of effective adult educator combined with activities designed to help readers reflect on and learn about themselves. The
point of Chapter 2 is that we, as adult educators, should make
systematic decisions about planning and implementing learning
activities based on the needs of our adult learners rather than
our own needs or limited repertoire of methods.

Chapter 3 is devoted to the topic of developing content
knowledge and transforming content knowledge into usable de-
signs for successful learning activities. To that end, procedural

task analysis, learning task analysis, an content analysis are described.

Conducting needs assessment of adult learners is described in Chapters 4 and 5. Chapter 4 is devoted to a discussion of the needs and characteristics of adult learners enhanced by a computer analogy of the learning process that illustrates the various needs and characteristics of adult learners. Strategies for conducting learner needs assessment are described in Chapter 5. Learner needs assessment can be accomplished by using your own store of knowledge, consulting experts, conducting a review of the literature, and applying direct data gathering techniques. The direct data gathering processes described are the use of interviews, groups, observation, standardized assessment instruments, locally constructed instruments, and surveys.

In Chapter 6 the discussion of gathering data is completed by describing learning contexts, the social, political, and economic realities in which the learning activities take place, and how to analyze them.

The next major topic of the book is the actual instructional design, described in Chapters 7 though 9. The information obtained through the processes described in Chapters 2 through 6 is use to develop goals and objectives (Chapter 7), learning activities (Chapter 8), and learner evaluation procedures (Chapter 9). Developing learning goals and objectives, described in Chapter 7, is not a straightforward process, but is one of decision making and compromise. At issue is balancing the strengths and needs of the adult educator, the demands of the content, the needs and characteristics of the adult learners, and the pressures of the learning contexts. These various factors are considered while developing the learning goals on which more specific statements, "objectives," can be based. Three types of objectives are discussed: behavioral, content, and problem centered.

In Chapter 8 developing learning activities is described. This consists of identifying the types of activities that are appropriate for the contents, the learners, and the contexts; developing the learning activities; and sequencing the activities to make for an effective flow of learning.

Learner evaluation is discussed in Chapter 9. Adult educators should consider a number of factors when developing evaluation procedures for their adult learners, including the purposes that evaluation will serve, what is important to evaluate, when to conduct the evaluation, and the methods to be used for evaluation.

The last major topic of the book, evaluating the instructional design plan, is addressed in Chapter 10. The plan should be evaluated before, during, and after its implementation to ensure that effective learning results. This will also help the adult educator becomes more proficient as an instructional designer and as a teacher of adults.

This is a "how-to" book written for the practitioner from a practitioner's point of view. To that end, the book is organized in such a way as to encourage its ready use for developing instructional activities for adult learners. It can be used in whole by those wanting to develop knowledge and skills in the entire instructional design process, or chapters and sections can be used independently by those desiring a review of certain instructional design concepts.

To enhance the transfer of the ideas presented in the text, the book contains figures, activities, exhibits, and examples. The figures help illustrate various points made in the text. The activities serve two purposes: (1) to encourage personal reflection and growth, and (2) to provide immediate opportunities for application of the instructional design process. The exhibits are used to highlight important information so that it is easily accessible. A running example in three parts was developed to show how instructional design can be used to plan learning activities. In the three examples, the process of training adult educators to be effective group discussion leaders is described. In the first example, identifying the tasks to be learned by group discussion leaders is described (Chapter 3). In the second example, developing appropriate learning goals and objectives is described (Chapter 7). In the third example, developing learning activities is described (Chapter 8).

Designing Instruction for Adult Learners presents a comprehensive, structured, and flexible plan to assist adult educators in preparing learning activities. The emphasis in this book is on a process that can be applied to a wide variety of settings, topics, learners, and adult educators. Adult educators often pride themselves on their ability to respond to learners' needs and to demonstrate effective interpersonal skills. When those qualities are coupled with systematic planning, the result will be highly effective and rewarding learning.

ACKNOWLEDGMENTS

No project of this size is undertaken without help. I would, therefore, like to thank the people who helped me in writing this book. First, I would like to express my thanks to Michael Galbraith—it was due to his willingness to listen to my ideas and his constant encouragement and patience that this project ever got started, let alone completed. The ideas for this book were first generated long ago in a class with William Dowling at Ohio State University. Thanks for the inspiration and all the help over the years. In addition, William Dowling took time out of his retirement to review the manuscript for the book and make many valuable suggestions for improving it. Carl Slaugenhaupt was indispensable during the early stages of this project. He spent many long hours helping me think through and refine the ideas set forth here. Trenton Ferro has given his time, ideas, and encouragement unstintingly. He also provided a helpful review of the manuscript. Thanks also goes to Peter Murk who made many good suggestions for improvement in a very thorough and speedy review of the manuscript. Debbie Sydow also did a nice job of reviewing the manuscript and made many helpful suggestions. Susan Hess's editing and sense of humor made the final version possible. And, of course, nothing would have happened without the typing assistance of Linda Butler and Corena Stefanik. In addition, Georgiana Jones and Ellen McDevitt proofread the final version and made many helpful suggestions. A big thanks also goes to the graduate students at Indiana University of Pennsylvania who helped me test and refine many of the ideas contained in this book.

No thanks would be complete without acknowledging Sandra Dean for her help in thinking through the ideas, reading endless drafts, constantly encouraging me, and her all-around help and support. Last, and certainly not least, I want to thank Jessie, Jenny, Penny, and Glennie. Jessie and Jenny contributed in so many ways through their constant help and unselfish behavior. Penny and Glennie, although they may not know it, are two of the best educators of adults I know.

THE AUTHOR

Gary J. Dean is Professor of Adult and Community Education at Indiana University of Pennsylvania (IUP) where he also serves as coordinator of the master's program in adult education and communications technology. He received his doctorate in adult education from The Ohio State University in 1987. His M.A. was also earned at Ohio State in 1982 and he graduated from Miami University (Ohio) with a B.S. in Education in 1972.

Dean has worked as a Drug and Alcohol Rehabilitation Counselor and Education Specialist for the U.S. Army, a career counselor, counselor supervisor, a trainer of career counselors for the Ohio Bureau of Employment Services, and as a graduate assistant developing training programs at the National Center for Research in Vocational Education.

Dean's interest in instructional design is based on his experience in developing training materials, including materials for the Ohio Bureau of Employment Services and for the Department of Defense. In addition, he has extensive consulting experience with community agencies, hospitals, government, and private industry.

Dean is also a coauthor (with Peter J. Murk and Tony Del Prete) of another Krieger publication in this series, *Enhancing Organizational Effectiveness in Adult and Community Education* (2000). In addition to instructional design and training, Dean's activities include the Student Literacy Corps, working with displaced workers, and serving as coeditor for the *PAACE Journal of Lifelong Learning*, the professional journal of the Pennsylvania Association for Adult Continuing Education.

CHAPTER 1

An Adult Education Model
for Instructional Design

Adult educators function in a great variety of educational settings, from recreational facilities to universities. In addition, Galbraith and Zelenak (1989) identified that adult educators have variety in training: on-the-job training, in-service training, and graduate programs in adult education. Many people who are functioning as adult educators do not even identify with the field (Galbraith & Zelenak, 1989). The upshot of this is that adult education occurs in many places through people who have diverse professional commitments and preparation for their role as adult educators. Common to all, however, is a need for systematic development of instructional knowledge, activities, and materials.

Langenbach (1988) reviewed several diverse models of curriculum development in adult education. He concluded that the "curricular commonplaces of goals, content, method, and evaluation are present in all of the models, but they do not receive similar treatment in each" (p. 209). These common elements identified by Langenbach provide the basis for the approach to instructional design used in this book. This model for instructional design is flexible and easy to use in the preparation of learning activities for adult learners. It may not be equally applicable to all adult education settings and purposes, but it provides guidelines for adult educators charged with developing effective learning activities and can be adapted to a great many settings.

The first of several topics addressed in this chapter is an overview of the instructional design model. Second, assumptions underlying the model are discussed. Third, common objections to the use of instructional design are explored.

OVERVIEW OF THE
INSTRUCTIONAL DESIGN MODEL

Instructional design is a systematic decision-making process that allows educators to identify the most important elements of the learning process and to make decisions about what will be the most effective way to plan and implement a learning activity. It has typically been used in technical training and school systems, but broader applications for instructional design can be employed in a great many areas of adult education.

A diagram of the model of instructional design developed in this book is portrayed in Figure 1.1., where the four boxes surrounding the circle represent a comprehensive approach to needs assessment, the first step in instructional design. Information gained in needs assessment is used to conduct the activities identified in the circle.

Four types of needs assessment are identified in the diagram. Box 1 represents assessing yourself as an adult educator. For novice adult educators, a thorough assessment of philosophical assumptions, experience, and skills is critical to future success. More experienced adult educators should include self-assessment as part of their ongoing professional development. Box 2 represents developing content knowledge, skills, and expertise. Box 3 focuses on assessing the needs of the adult learners. This is what many educators think of when needs assessment is discussed. Box 4 represents assessing the learning contexts: the social, political, and economic settings in which learning takes place. The purpose of the diagram is to emphasize that adult educators should perform needs assessments in all four areas prior to developing goals, objectives, learning activities, and evaluation. They must be aware, before beginning to develop the actual instructional plan, of themselves as adult educators, their content knowledge, the learners' needs, and the political, social, and economic situations that affect the learning process.

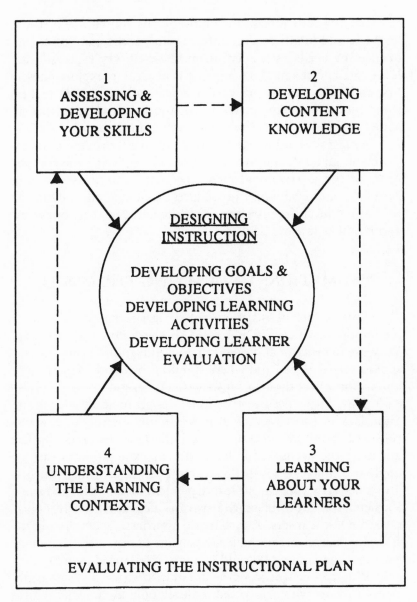

Figure 1.1 Designing Instruction for Adult Learners

Begin with yourself, then move to the content, next to the learners, and finally to the contexts—this is the appropriate sequence for needs assessment in most situations, especially for less experienced adult educators. It is natural to explore oneself first and move steadily outward in scope and horizon. In reality, these four areas interact with one another, and educators of adults constantly move back and forth among them.

Armed with information gained from a thorough needs assessment, an adult educator can proceed to develop the components of the instructional plan: goals and objectives, learning activities, and evaluation procedures. Last, the adult educator reflects on the entire process of developing the instructional plan and modifies it as needed.

ASSUMPTIONS UNDERLYING THE MODEL

This model of instructional design is based on several assumptions which are addressed in the following questions: Why use instructional design in adult education? Who can and should use it? When and where should it be used? Why is there a need for a new model of instructional design?

Why do we need instructional design in adult education? First, lack of formal training in developing instructional materials and activities can result in activities and materials that do not meet the needs of the learners. For example, it is easy to apply too much or too little structure in the learning process. Too much structure can stifle independent or sophisticated adult learners. Too little structure frustrates dependent or unsophisticated adult learners. A systematic approach to developing instruction, based on thorough assessments of instructors, content, learners, and contexts should result in a balanced approach.

Who can benefit from the use of instructional design processes? Anyone who is involved in developing learning activities. Adult educators with little or no formal training can increase the quality of their instructional activities and materials. More experienced adult educators can improve existing instructional activities or develop activities in new content areas.

When and where should instructional design be used? Instructional design has been associated with technical training and curriculum development in school systems. Application of instructional design can be broadened to include recreational adult education, professional development, occupational training, personal development, graduate education, and more. Instructional design is a tool to be employed whenever systematic planning for learning activities is desired.

Why is there a need for a new model of instructional design? Traditional models of instructional design are often complicated systems that employ technical language and difficult procedures. In addition, traditional models are usually content driven and not easily adapted to numerous settings or varieties of learners. The instructional design model outlined in this book is a straightforward approach with a minimum of technical language. It is intended to be flexible in its application and responsive to settings, learners, adult educators, content, and contexts.

OBJECTIONS TO USING INSTRUCTIONAL DESIGN

Some objections by adult educators to the adoption of instructional design highlight the legitimate limitations of the process, while others can be adequately addressed.

One objection is that too much expertise is involved. Some people feel it is inappropriate to expect an adult educator to be an expert in content and in instructional design. It is true that adult educators must master new skills to employ instructional design effectively. In most cases these include writing learning goals and objectives, planning learning activities, and preparing learner evaluations. Adult educators have responsibilities in both areas: content and process expertise. Content expertise is knowledge and skill in the content to be learned by the adult learner. Process expertise is knowledge and skill in how to help adults learn the content. Knowledge and skill in using instructional design are a part of the adult educator's process expertise.

A second objection to using instructional design is that it

is too time consuming. Using instructional design will require more up-front time; however, it will result in learning activities which are more carefully planned. The end result is more effective learning and less time wasted in the long run. As a consequence, both educators and learners will have a better experience.

A third objection is the inflexibility of traditional approaches to instructional design. Many of these approaches focus on content only and employ complex task analysis procedures. An approach responsive to the needs of learners, adult educators, the contexts, and content can be much more flexible and applicable in a greater variety of settings. For instance, detailed planning does not preclude mid-course corrections. In fact, adult educators can use the principles of instructional design to identify and troubleshoot problems in the early stages and make mid-course corrections as needed.

Still other adult educators argue that instructional design is primarily intended for group instruction and inhibits responsiveness to individual learners in the group. This objection is more properly placed on the mind-set of the adult educator. Instructional design provides a blueprint for conducting learning activities, not rigid rules which preclude modification of learning objectives, activities, and assessments to accommodate individual learners.

A fifth objection to the use of instructional design is that it prevents taking advantage of unintended outcomes; determining learning objectives in advance does not allow for spontaneous learning. Again, this difficulty is more a matter of adult educators' style than one of instructional design. Any learning activity implemented in an inflexible manner will discourage spontaneous or unanticipated learning. If the adult educator is flexible and chooses to implement instructional design in a flexible manner, then unanticipated learning can be recognized and encouraged.

A sixth objection of adult educators is that behavioral learning objectives, which are often considered an integral part of instructional design, do not account for all of the varieties of learning which occur. Although all demonstrations of learning can be stated in behavioral terms, it does not always make sense to do so. This model suggests that sometimes it does not make sense to use specifically stated behavioral objectives; not all outcomes of learning need to be reduced to behavioral terms.

Adult educators also argue that preplanning does not involve learners in developing, implementing, or evaluating learning goals and objectives. If developing the instructional plan is kept as the prerogative of the adult educator, then this is true. However, learners can be involved in some or all aspects of the instructional design process. This may help them develop a sense of ownership and encourage them to tailor learning activities to meet their specific needs.

Some adult educators also may believe that instructional design, based on behavioral concepts of learning, is incompatible with their beliefs about adult education, adults, and learning. This objection is actually two arguments. First, instructional design is incompatible with certain outcomes in adult education. No particular outcomes, however, are advocated through the use of instructional design. Instructional design is a tool that educators employ to achieve a wide range of learning outcomes. Instructional design can help people learn facts, concepts, skills, and attitudes, and aid them in problem solving. The second argument is that instructional design, a behavioristic approach to structuring learning, is inconsistent with humanistic approaches to adult education. When instructional design is used to manipulate learners without their knowledge or against their will, then this claim is true. When the rights of learners are respected and when learners engage in learning of their own free will, then the use of specific learning goals and objectives based on a thorough needs assessment—the key components of instructional design—can be compatible with humanistic outcomes.

SUMMARY

Instructional design is a decision-making process used to plan and develop instructional materials and activities. This model presents in logical sequence the four general activities needed for comprehensive instructional design: assessing needs, determining educational goals and objectives, designing learning activities, and developing evaluation. In practice, instructional design is an iterative process and involves doing a little of each of these activities at the same time.

Although many adult educators do not understand instructional design or see its relevance to their daily activity of helping adults learn, many adult educators and learners could benefit from systematic planning. The commitment of time and energy necessary to employ instructional design pays off in more effective and efficient learning.

CHAPTER 2

Assessing and Developing Your Skills

Adult educators often rely only on techniques with which they are comfortable, even when the outcome may not be best for the learners. In addition, adult educators often make educational decisions unconsciously rather than with intention and foresight. If we are to effectively help adults learn, then our basic decisions as adult educators must be made consciously and knowledgeably.

What do we need to know about ourselves in order to better prepare for our roles as adult educators? The process of instructional design encompasses the whole of the teaching-learning transaction from initial planning to final evaluation. In this chapter the attributes, assumptions, styles, skills, and experiences of adult educators that affect decisions about planning and facilitating learning are discussed.

ATTRIBUTES OF SUCCESSFUL ADULT EDUCATORS

The many lists developed to describe effective adult educators may, at first glance, look intimidating, especially if we see them as standards to judge our worth. It is more helpful to view the various lists as goals which adult educators can use for professional development, and as guidelines to help us reflect on our strengths and weaknesses. We each possess qualities upon which we can draw and build.

Draves (1984) suggested that adult educators should love their subject, desire to share it, and be competent in it. Seaman and Fellenz (1989) identified needs manifested by teachers of adults which may impact on their teaching: popularity, pride of accomplishment, self-confidence, desire to be helpful, expression of personality, self-improvement, and financial gain. Seaman and Fellenz also stated that administrators and teachers must be realistic about whether or not all of the teachers' needs can be met. In addition, teachers must learn how to communicate those needs to others, especially to administrators and adult learners.

Grabowski (1976) identified a set of competencies that adult educators should have. He stated that adult educators should understand the motivation and participation patterns of adult learners, understand and provide for their needs, be knowledgeable in the theory and practice of adult learners, know the community and its needs, and know how to use various methods and techniques of instruction. They should also be good communicators and listeners, know how to locate and use educational materials, be open minded and allow adults to pursue their own interests, continue their own education, and be able to evaluate and appraise a program.

Dean and Ferro (1991) provided the following list of characteristics of good adult educators: a belief that adults can change and learn, enthusiasm about both the learners and the topic, patience and willingness to listen to others carefully, knowledge of the topic, ability to articulate material clearly, flexibility, openness, and a sense of humor.

Though critical for the success of an adult learner, the intangible qualities identified above are difficult to measure. How can you tell if you possess enough of the right qualities? Start by asking other people what they think of you as an adult educator—ask your students, other adult educators, and administrators. Another approach is outlined in Activity 2.1. Identifying a personal list of qualities may be difficult, even painful, but is highly beneficial for both the adult educator and the learners.

ACTIVITY 2.1
Assessing Your Qualities as an Adult Educator*

---

1. Recall a situation in which you helped someone or a group of people learn something. Describe the situation.

2. Identify at least one thing you did which worked well in that situation. Explain why it worked.

3. Identify at least one thing you wish you had done better or differently in that situation. Explain why it did not work.

4. Based on your response to items 1, 2, and 3, identify the qualities you possess that make you a good adult educator.

5. Compare the qualities identified in item 4 to the lists discussed in the text. Which additional qualities do you need to develop? What can you do to enhance the qualities you possess? Which additional qualities do you need to develop?

6. Have others, such as students and colleagues, assess you by responding to the questions in this exercise as well. Let them respond anonymously so they will give honest and useful feedback.

*Adapted from Dean and Ferro (1991).

ASSUMPTIONS ABOUT
LEARNING AND LEARNERS

Our philosophical assumptions affect the way we treat learners and plan and conduct learning activities. The most compelling reason for getting in touch with our philosophical orientations is that our behavior is affected by them whether we are aware of it or not.

Several schemas have been used to conceptualize philosophical orientations in adult education. Brookfield (1989) suggested three primary paradigms from which facilitators of adult education operate: the behaviorist, the humanist, and the critical. Darkenwald and Merriam (1982) enumerated five philosophical orientations for adult educators, including cultivation of the intellect, individual self-actualization, personal and social improvement, social transformation, and organizational effectiveness. Elias and Merriam (1995) identified six basic philosophical orientations which appear to guide most adult educators. These include liberal, progressive, behaviorist, humanist, radical, and analytical adult education. Each orientation to adult education is based on different assumptions about learners, learning, and the purpose of education. What we do as adult educators is directly affected by our assumptions.

To explore the reasons why adult educators educate adults, we must divide the various reasons into categories for easier understanding. There are two main types of reasons for engaging in adult education: how we personally benefit from being an adult educator and what we believe is important about being an adult educator (Dean, 2001). The second type of motivation is divided into four categories: to help individuals, to enhance organizational effectiveness, to improve society, and to educate for the sake of education. As is readily noticed, these various motivations are not mutually exclusive. Nor is it true that any one person can easily be pigeonholed in only one category. As Merriam and Brockett (1997) point out, any one person may employ an eclectic approach and draw a philosophical foundation for adult education from more than one category. Also, our motivations may change given the setting in which we operate. Likewise, our motivation to engage in our careers varies over time. Our motivations for working at the age of 20 are not the same as they are at mid-career or later in life. It can be readily seen that the motivations to work, to teach, and to be an adult educator are a fluid business at best with a constantly changing mix of feelings, values, beliefs, and assumptions. This underscores the constant need for self-assessment to help us to identify our values, beliefs, and assumptions as we practice the art and science of adult education.

One way to identify philosophical orientation is to ask:

What are the most important goals of adult education? Goals can be identified at societal, institutional, instructional, and individual levels. Examples of societal goals include the need for social change, the need for the development or use of new technology, or the need to address social problems and issues. Examples of institutional goals include expanding or retrenching the organization and adapting to a changing organizational environment. Instructional goals are those specified as the desired learning outcomes of a course, workshop, or learning activity. At the individual level, goals which lead to the acquisition of knowledge, skills, and attitudes; career advancement or change; personal development; and escape are often identified.

At all levels, philosophical orientation determines how goals are defined. For instance, the "goals" acquisition of knowledge, skills, and attitudes may mean, from a radical orientation, empowerment, developing independence, and freedom from oppression. From the humanistic orientation, self-actualization and, ultimately, transpersonal experiences and understanding may be the goals. From the liberal perspective, it may mean developing an understanding and appreciation of one's cultural heritage, and from the critical sense it may mean adult learners acquire the increased ability to "scrutinize critically the values, beliefs, and assumptions, they have uncritically assimilated from the dominant culture" (Brookfield, 1989, p. 205).

Activity 2.2, Assessing Your Assumptions about Teaching and Learning, provides an opportunity to reflect on your philosophical orientation. Because change is fundamental to the process of learning, it is useful to begin by identifying your beliefs about change.

Although there are no ready or even correct answers to the questions in Activity 2.2, attempting to answer them provides insight into our assumptions regarding teaching and learning and our role in it as adult educators.

As a system for developing learning activities and materials, instructional design appears to imply a certain philosophical viewpoint, and use of instructional design must include at least some acceptance of behaviorist principles. This does not imply, however, that instructional design processes are antithetical to

14   DESIGNING INSTRUCTION FOR ADULT LEARNERS

ACTIVITY 2.2
Assessing Your Assumptions
about Teaching and Learning

---

1. Do you believe people can change? If so, under what conditions do they change?

2. How easily can people change?

3. What should be the role of adult educators in helping others to learn and change?

4. What are the best methods or techniques for helping different people learn and change?

5. How can it be determined that people have changed?

6. What are your responsibilities in helping people change?

7. What do you believe are the goals of adult education on the societal, institutional, instructional, and individual levels?

8. What is your role as an adult educator in achieving these goals?

9. How do you contribute to these goals and purposes?

---

humanistic, radical, critical, liberal, or any other philosophical bases of adult education.

Gagne, Briggs, and Wager (1988) stated that as "scientists, investigators are basically interested in explaining how learning takes place. In other words, their interest is in relating both the internal and external parts of a learning situation to the process of behavior change called learning" (p. 6). The behavior changes are linked to internal processes in which learning is conceived as information processing. When the internal processes of information processing are taken into account as leading to behavior change, then instruction becomes "a deliberately arranged set of external events designed to support internal learning processes" (p. 11), which leads to the desired behaviors.

While observable behavior is intrinsic to instructional design processes, it is only part of the recognized learning process. Instructional design takes into account these internal information processing aspects of learning as well as the observable outcomes of the learning process. Any purpose of adult education can be supported through instructional design. Instructional design is a method to achieve an end, not an end in itself.

TEACHING STYLES AND SKILLS

How an adult educator helps others to learn is inextricably linked with how he or she learns best. Many adult educators as children were successful in school; they were able to identify a comfortable niche where they were successful. This niche was defined by relationships with teachers, other students, the school and community, and the subjects studied. The first step to a better handle on teaching style is to understand the various approaches to learning.

Knox (1986) stated that "teaching style consists of the characteristic ways in which you help adults learn" (p. 41). He further stated that "teaching tends to be quite intuitive and implicit, largely reflecting the instructor's personal qualities and habits" (p. 41). Teaching style, according to Knox, consists of two aspects, responsiveness and procedures. Responsiveness consists of the ways in which adult educators should respond to the learners. He stated that adult educators should (1) "be supportive and encourage participants to be resources for the learning of others as well as active agents of their own learning"; (2) "accommodate participant needs and expectations that fit program purposes"; (3) "let participants know early where their reasons and program purposes match, and help them seek resources and assistance to meet needs that some learners may want to pursue beyond your program"; (4) "help participants understand their characteristics related to learning and will provide options for individuals as well as the group"; and (5) "allow for the selection of examples, concepts, and procedures likely to be helpful to the participants at their current stage of development" (p. 44).

Conti (1990) developed the Principles of Adult Learning Scale to measure the degree to which adult educators incorporate adult teaching and learning principles into their teaching methods. Conti defines teaching style as "the distinct qualities displayed by a teacher that are persistent from situation to situation regardless of the content" (p. 80). He further stated that to "identify one's style, the total atmosphere created by the teacher's views on learning and the teacher's approach to teaching must be examined" (p. 81).

Although teaching style defines an adult educator's typical behaviors when helping others learn, there are also specific skills and experiences we acquire as adult educators. Draves (1984) listed several skills of a good adult educator: having effective listening skills, being able to help insecure learners, being able to handle situations involving incorrect learner actions, using supportive actions and words, and possessing a sense of humor.

Knox (1986) suggests the importance of self-assessment of adult educator effectiveness in the following areas:

- Balancing presentation and learner involvement;
- Encouraging active learning;
- Assisting learners in their search for meaning;
- Using a variety of teaching methods;
- Establishing proper learning climates at the beginning, middle, and end of a program;
- Attending to affective and cognitive objectives;
- Displaying proper interpersonal relations;
- Helping learners make past and future connections to their current learning;
- Responding to the needs and purposes of the learners;
- Combining support with challenges for the learners;
- Providing models for the learners;
- Developing self-direction in learners;
- Developing confidence in learners;

- Providing feedback to learners; and
- Being flexible in implementing plans.

Zemke and Zemke (1981) suggested a number of activities which they feel are effective for helping adults learn. These include the following:

- Develop a physically and psychologically comfortable learning environment;
- Be aware of learners' self-esteem and ego needs;
- Help learners clarify and articulate expectations;
- Use learners' life experiences in the classroom;
- Use open-ended questions and other techniques to encourage learner participation;
- Elicit feedback from the learners' course progress and learner expectations;
- Balance teacher-centered control and learner control;
- Protect minority opinion;
- Help learners transfer classroom knowledge and skills to real-life situations; and
- Use theories of learning as resources, not as rules.

Galbraith (1998) divided skills that adult educators should have into two categories: program planning skills and teaching and learning transaction skills. Program planning skills are conducting needs assessments, conducting context analysis, setting educational objectives, organizing learning activities, and preparing evaluation. Teaching and learning transaction skills are establishing an educational climate and providing challenging teaching and learning transactions.

A transactional process is one in which facilitators and learners engage "in an active, challenging, collaborative, critically reflective, and transforming educational encounter" (Galbraith, 1991, p. 1). According to Galbraith the adult educator should adhere to the following six principles to develop a transactional learning situation:

1. Adopt an appropriate philosophical orientation;

2. Recognize and understand the diversity of adult learners;

ACTIVITY 2.3
Assessing Teaching Styles and Skills

---

1. I am most comfortable teaching when . . .

2. The degree of control needed in teaching is . . .

3. I feel the proper relationship between teacher and learners is . . .

4. The techniques I use most often are . . .

5. The techniques I am most comfortable with are . . .

6. The techniques I am least comfortable with are . . .

7. Learning is most exciting when . . .

8. I make learning exciting by . . .

9. Changes I want to make in my teaching are . . .

---

3. Create a conducive psychological climate for learning;

4. Create challenging teaching and learning situations;

5. Foster critical reflections and praxis; and

6. Encourage independence.

Margolis and Bell (1986) identified a number of strategies an effective trainer should display during training: making arrangements for the training setting, maintaining a learning climate, making presentations, giving instructions, monitoring individual and subgroup tasks, managing the reporting process, managing learning activities, and determining what to do when the training is over.

Several questions are posed in Activity 2.3, Assessing Teaching Styles and Skills, that are helpful in the process of taking a critical look at one's experiences and skills as an adult educator and identifying and reflecting on one's teaching style. Comparing your responses to the items in Activity 2.3 with the ideas of the different authors presented in this chapter also will be useful.

EXPERIENCE AND SKILLS
WITH INSTRUCTIONAL DESIGN

It is interesting to note that in all the lists of attributes of good adult educators reviewed in this chapter, none have mentioned the process of planning or instructional design. It would seem natural that good teaching begins with good preparation. It is important to analyze your previous experience with instructional design so that you can determine how it will be enhanced in the future.

Zemke and Zemke (1981) identified a number of important guidelines for adult educators in the role of trainers and human resource developers in organizations. For curriculum design they identified, by implication, the following points:

- Focus on single theory or single concept courses instead of survey courses.
- Help adults integrate new information with old for more efficient learning.
- Avoid fast-paced or unusual learning tasks when possible.
- Allow the adult learners time to complete activities.
- Determine if the new information is in concert with or conflict with organizational values.
- Allow for different life stages and value sets of learners; concepts need to be explained from several viewpoints, value sets, and developmental stages.
- Allow for self-directed and self-designed learning.
- Emphasize how-to and application in instruction.

Useful questions to ask yourself when you reflect on your experience with planning learning activities include: When is extensive planning required? When is minimal planning adequate? When extensive planning is required, what processes or systems have been helpful? How difficult and time consuming is it to plan learning activities? Is the end result worth the time invested?

SUMMARY

Instructional design is a decision-making process which is affected by the adult educator's beliefs, needs, skills, experiences, and weaknesses. Instructional design, in turn, affects all aspects of the teaching and learning transaction. This chapter focused on helping adult educators develop and relate self-knowledge to instructional design. First, basic attributes of successful adult educators were identified to help both novice and experienced educators engage in self-reflection. Second, philosophical orientations of adult educators as they relate to instructional design were explored. Instructional design is a tool for realizing any philosophical and educational goals; however, philosophical orientation will influence emphasis placed on the method of incorporating instructional design into the teaching and learning process. Third, teaching styles and skills were explored to help identify how you teach, your preferences for teaching, and your specific teaching skills. The selection and use of specific skills are often limited by the adult educator's experience and comfort level. Last, experiences with instructional design were considered to help you determine how you can use it more successfully in the future.

CHAPTER 3

Developing Content Knowledge

This chapter explores how content expertise is developed. The primary focus is on analyzing the subject matter to be learned. This analysis provides the raw data for developing learning goals and objectives. Three methods of analysis are discussed: procedural task analysis, learning task analysis, and content analysis.

Subject matter or content expertise is often the sole criterion for hiring a person to teach in adult education. Emphasizing the importance of content expertise, Knox (1986) stated that content mastery "refers to all aspects of the proficiencies to be acquired or enhanced by participants. These include knowledge, psychomotor skills, and attitudes" (pp. 40–41). According to Knox, a high level of content mastery: (1) focuses instructors on important aspects of the subject, (2) helps adult educators select teaching methods and techniques, (3) provides standards against which participants can compare their proficiencies, (4) provides adult educators the freedom to be flexible and responsive to the learners, and (5) helps adult educators develop educational objectives.

Some adult educators gain content expertise through formal education, while others pick up skills as an avocation, and still others develop their expertise on the job. Sometimes these methods fall to provide adult educators with all of the content expertise needed to develop an effective instructional package. Adult educators can acquire additional information by consulting experts, observing people, reviewing written documents such as position descriptions or job procedures, or learning how to do the activities themselves. Each approach requires a different level of commitment, time, interest, and resources that determine which approach will be most useful to the educator.

Seels and Glasgow (1990) identified three processes as common elements in most instructional design models: needs analysis, task analysis, and instructional analysis. These are decision-making processes in which the instructional designer "moves back and forth among the different types of analysis because analysis is an iterative process. The process consists of collecting information for a specific purpose, analyzing the data, and making decisions based on that data" (p. 109). Needs analysis is defined as acquiring relevant information about the learners; task analysis is learning about the tasks to be learned; and instructional analysis is developing the instructional processes which will be used. In this book, these three processes are refined into five steps: (1) identifying tasks and skills to be learned, (2) developing goals and objectives, (3) sequencing goals and objectives, (4) developing learning activities to meet the goals and objectives, and (5) developing assessment procedures. The first step, identifying tasks and skills to be learned, or "task analysis," is the subject of this chapter.

A few basic terms are necessary to understand task analysis. *Tasks* are the specific components of an activity to be learned. *Skills* are what the learner must do to master the tasks.

Learning objectives are developed from the tasks and skills identified. Objectives are stated in behavioral terms, and two types of objectives commonly are identified: *target objectives* (outcomes) and *enabling objectives* (those learned en route to the outcomes). A *goal* is a general statement of a desired outcome of the learning process. A goal can usually be divided into several objectives and need not be stated in behavioral terms, but should fit into one or more of the learning domains.

Learning outcomes or *domains* are the result of the learning process. Gagne and Briggs (1979) identified five categories of learning outcomes: (1) intellectual skills, (2) cognitive strategies, (3) verbal information, (4) attitudes, and (5) psychomotor skills. A less complex classification system consists of the domains of cognitive knowledge, attitudes, and psychomotor skills. In this less complex system, there are two levels of cognitive learning outcomes: a more basic level of information acquisition and a more advanced level of the application of information for problem solving. Learning outcomes provide the basis for understanding how goals, objectives, skills, and tasks fit together.

Learning activities are experiences used to achieve learning objectives and goals. Each learning activity can meet one or more learning objectives, and several learning activities usually contribute to achieving a learning goal.

A *lesson, course, workshop,* or *program* is a sequence of learning activities designed to reach one or more goals. For example, a course entitled, "Facilitating Adult Learning" may include goals such as becoming familiar with adult teaching and learning strategies, developing competence in using those strategies, and determining the appropriate strategies for different situations.

IDENTIFYING TASKS AND SKILLS TO BE LEARNED

Instructional designers often refer to one or more processes for acquiring the content knowledge necessary for developing instructional activities and materials. These processes are usually referred to as task analysis. Gagne, Briggs, and Wager (1988) identified two types of task analysis: procedural task analysis and learning task analysis. Cranton (1989) also identified two types of task analysis: task analysis and procedural analysis. Seels and Glasgow (1990) referred only to task analysis, but specified different skills to be learned and specific processes for identifying the tasks of each skill.

It can readily be seen that there is little agreement on the use of terms among instructional designers. To create some continuity, the terminology described by Gagne, Briggs, and Wager (1988) is used here: procedural task analysis is the identification and analysis of the tasks to be learned; learning task analysis is the identification and analysis of the skills required to master each task. The distinction between these two processes can be difficult to make but is vital to effective instructional design. A third process, content analysis, is also discussed. Content analysis is often thought of as a way to develop content mastery tests, but it can also be used to determine course, workshop, lesson, or program content.

PROCEDURAL TASK ANALYSIS

For Gagne, Briggs, and Wager (1988) the outcome of a procedural task analysis is identification of "the steps in the process of performing a task or skill" (p. 143). The authors further identified two kinds of information that result from procedural task analysis: (1) a clear description of the target objectives, and (2) identification of steps that might not otherwise be obvious. A thorough procedural task analysis includes identification of target objectives and of the level of performance required for each.

Procedural task analysis is used when the material to be learned is a specific skill or series of skills. Examples of situations in which procedural task analysis is appropriate include learning to operate machines, learning physical skills, learning procedures or routines on the job, and learning techniques or skills to solve problems. Any content to be learned which can be divided into tasks can be analyzed using procedural task analysis. Procedural task analysis is useful when the learning outcomes involve solving problems, displaying attitudes, or demonstrating psychomotor skills.

Procedural task analysis can be accomplished with a series of steps. First, clearly and completely describe the activity to be learned. Second, based on that description, identify the tasks of the activity. The list of tasks should be as detailed as possible. Tasks can always be discarded later as too elementary for the learners, but the failure to include a key task can create difficulties. Third, sequence the tasks to reflect the order of activities as they occur in the natural setting.

Tasks can be identified by observing the activity, either directly or with a video tape recorder; consulting experts who can identify the key tasks to be learned; and employing a flow chart. A flow chart is useful to identify all tasks to be performed in sequence and any decisions to be made while doing the tasks.

LEARNING TASK ANALYSIS

According to Gagne, Briggs, and Wager (1988), learning task analysis is the identification of skills required to learn each task identified through procedural task analysis. Two types of skills are identified through the learning task analysis: new skills to be learned and prerequisite skills. New skills are the object of the learning activities to be designed. Prerequisite skills must be mastered before the new skills can be learned. For example, a learner must have mastered basic math before attempting algebra, just as a counselor must be an effective listener before learning intervention skills. Identifying prerequisite skills helps avoid the disasters caused by learning activities that are either too advanced or too simple. A thorough assessment of relevant learner needs and identification of learner competencies will yield an understanding of the learners' current level of knowledge and skills.

CONTENT ANALYSIS

Content analysis is useful when material is not easily divided into tasks and when acquiring information is the primary intended learning outcome. Content analysis is really a special case of procedural task analysis. All learning activities can ultimately be reduced to specific behaviors. In many situations, however, it does not make sense to do so. When specific behaviors are too discrete or mundane and the emphasis is on content acquisition rather than skills, then content analysis can provide a useful tool for determining what needs to be learned.

A key element in conducting content analysis is identifying content domains. According to Murphy and Davidshofer

(1991), content domains consist of boundaries and structure. The boundaries define where one content domain ends and other content domains begin. The structure of a content domain is defined by the distribution of topics within the content domain. For example, a content domain for a course on adult learners may consist of theories of adult development (30 percent of the course), theories of adult learning (30 percent of the course), and other psychological, sociological, and physiological characteristics of adult learners (40 percent of the course). The content domain boundaries are defined by the concept "adult learner" and the content domain structure is determined by the relative weight and time given to each topic within the course.

TASK ANALYSIS: AN EXAMPLE

An example of procedural task analysis, learning task analysis and content analysis illustrates how they can be used in real-life situations. Exhibit 3.1 lists the tasks and skills required of an effective adult education group discussion. Column 1 represents a procedural task analysis; the actual tasks required of a group discussion leader are listed. There are several methods which could have been used to identify the tasks: (1) observing effective discussion group leaders, (2) consulting experts on group processes, (3) reviewing the literature, or (4) a combination of these approaches.

Column 2 represents a learning task analysis; the knowledge and skills required to perform each task are identified. The status of each item listed in Column 2 as new or prerequisite learning would then be determined. If items are new learning, then other prerequisite learning required to master these concepts will also need to be identified. If items are prerequisite learning, then they would not be incorporated in learning objectives and activities, but learner competency should be assessed, not assumed.

Content analysis will identify the content domains of each component labeled as "knowledge" in column 2. For example, a content analysis of "group dynamics" identifies boundaries

EXHIBIT 3.1
Some Tasks and Skills of Group Discussion Leaders

1. Procedural Task Analysis (Tasks of a Group Leader)	2. Learning Task Analysis (Knowledge, Attitudes, and Skills Required for the Tasks)
Arrange group setting.	Knowledge of group dynamics.
Help group set goals.	Knowledge of content being discussed, group processing skills.
Help group members define roles.	Knowledge of group roles and processes, interpersonal skills.
Encourage participation of some group members.	Interpersonal skills, belief in the value of participation, knowledge of group roles and processes.
Control participation of some group members.	Interpersonal skills, respect for the rights of others, knowledge of group roles and processes.
Help group stay on course.	Knowledge of group roles and processes, knowledge of specific group facilitation techniques.
Help group achieve goals and bring closure.	Knowledge of group roles and processes, knowledge of specific group facilitation techniques.

(what is meant by group dynamics in this situation) and structure (what topics would be covered in a presentation on group dynamics).

SUMMARY

Developing content knowledge often depends on a complex but important task or content analysis. There are three crucial steps in this process: (1) identifying tasks and skills to be learned; (2) translating tasks and skills into learning goals and objectives; and (3) identifying goals and objectives as belonging to one or more learning domains. Identification of all of the tasks to be learned produces the core information needed for developing goal statements, writing specific objectives, developing learning activities, and, ultimately, developing assessment procedures for the learners. The task analysis information, however, is only really useful when considered in conjunction with the adult educator's self-assessment, needs assessment of the learners, and assessment of the learning contexts.

CHAPTER 4

Learner Needs and Characteristics

Learner needs and how to assess them are very complex topics. Because of this complexity, the discussion in this book has been divided into two chapters. This chapter describes learner needs and characteristics, and Chapter 5 is devoted to understanding how to assess these needs and characteristics. The discussion in this chapter begins with an exploration of needs and motivation. Following this, a discussion of learner characteristics is presented in which various characteristics that influence learning are identified. Then the interrelationships among these characteristics are described using a computer analogy of the learning process.

Volumes have been written about adults, just from a learning perspective. The discussion in this book is necessarily limited, but there are many other resources for a more detailed exploration of adult learning. One of the more comprehensive books which explores adult learning is Merriam and Cafarella's (1998) *Learning in Adulthood*. Another useful resource is Tennant's (1988) *Psychology and Adult Learning*. Both books offer a more comprehensive and detailed view of adult learning than is provided here.

LEARNER NEEDS

The term *learner characteristics* is used to describe that mixed bag of physical, cognitive, and affective factors that make up the human being. Learner needs are a subset of learner characteristics inextricably linked with motivation. According to

Wlodkowski (1986) a need "is a condition experienced by the individual as an internal force that leads the person to move in the direction of a goal" (p. 47). Wlodkowski further stated:

> Most psychologists concerned with learning and education use the word motivation to describe those processes that can (a) arouse and instigate behavior, (b) give direction or purpose to behavior, (c) continue to allow behavior to persist, and (d) lead to choosing or performing a particular behavior. (p. 2)

As is indicated by Wlodkowski in his discussion, the boundaries between motivation and need are unclear. The terms can be differentiated, however, by saying that a need is a condition that creates the opportunity for behavior, and motivation is the force behind the behavior aimed at satisfying the need. People are also subject to many conflicting motivations (Dean, 1993). A problem for some adult learners is that there are issues other than learning in their lives that may interfere with their participation and success in adult education. For example, some women enrolled in adult basic education may not have the support of their families for furthering their education. If the women have a need both for self-improvement and to maintain harmony at home, then they face conflicting needs. If they feel it is more important to meet their need for self-improvement, then their need for harmony at home will have to be diminished or met in some other way. On the other hand, if their need for harmony at home is greater than their need for self-improvement, then they may give up attending school.

Monette (1977) has suggested that there are four categories of needs as they relate to adult education. Two of those categories are relevant for instructional design: felt or expressed needs and normative needs. Felt or expressed needs are recognized by the learner, and often prompt participation in voluntary adult education programs. Normative needs represent a gap between a desired and an actual level of knowledge, attitude, or skill. Examples of normative needs are poor job performance due to lack of skill or inability to pass a test due to lack of knowledge.

Knowles (1980) posited two kinds of needs that have meaning for adult educators, basic human needs and educational needs. Basic human needs "have relevance to education in that they provide the deep motivating springs for learning, and that they prescribe certain conditions that the educators must take into account if they are to help people learn" (p. 88). Knowles further explained that an educational need:

> is something people ought to learn for their own good, the good of an organization, or for the good of society. It is the gap between their present level of competencies and a higher level required for effective performance as defined by themselves, their organization, or society. (p. 88)

Like Monette's normative needs, educational needs for Knowles are a gap between present level of competencies and the level required for effective performance.

Instructional design, for the most part, has been used to respond to normative needs. In these cases, education or training is perceived to be the way to close the gap between current behavior and desired behavior. This scenario implies that needs are usually determined by someone other than the learner, but instructional design can also respond to the felt needs of learners as well. When this is the case, learners themselves can be more involved in the process of developing goals, objectives, and learning activities. Barriers to participation can stifle or disrupt an adult's attempt to satisfy learning needs. While reducing barriers is usually considered a programmatic concern and not an instructional one, carefully designed learning activities can strengthen motivation for participation by reducing the barriers which occur during learning.

LEARNER CHARACTERISTICS

Cross (1981) provided a framework for understanding the characteristics of adult learners. Her model consists of two categories: personal characteristics and situational characteristics. Personal characteristics are physiology and aging, sociocultural and life stages, and psychological and developmental stages. Situational characteristics consist of part-time versus full-time status and voluntary versus compulsory learning. Using Cross's model, adult educators can identify physical, cognitive, and affective characteristics which affect the participation and performance of their learners.

Translating general concepts into specific characteristics to assess can be difficult. The fact is, however, that adult educators functioning as program planners, instructional designers, and facilitators of learning are faced daily with the task of identifying the characteristics and needs of their adult learners. A partial list of adult learner characteristics is presented in Exhibit 4.1.

The list is quite long, but it is not necessary to assess all characteristics for each adult learner in each learning situation. Figure 4.1, The Learning Process: A Computer Analogy, is an attempt to show the relationships among the various characteristics listed in Exhibit 4.1 and how each affects the learning process. Figure 4.1 is adapted from an earlier version of the computer analogy developed by Dean and Kalamas (1987).

The computer analogy displays the learning process so that educators can identify the individual components of the learning process and examine the interrelationships among them. Box 1 represents stimuli presented to the learner. The stimuli consists of the adult educator, the learning activities and materials, the learning methods used, and other competing or distracting stimuli from the environment. All are part of a complex set of stimuli to which the learner must learn to respond selectively.

Boxes 2–5 represent the learner. The physiological and psychological processes of acquiring, storing, processing, and retrieving information and responding to stimuli are listed in boxes 2–4. Learners become aware of all stimuli through their five senses—visual, auditory, haptic (touch), olfactory (smell), and gustatory (taste). These are listed in box 2. Box 3 shows the complex and much researched cognitive processes of information storage, processing, and retrieval. Two areas, memory and cognitive styles, have shown particular relevance for understanding learning. Box 4 represents the ways learners respond— by writing, speaking, or moving.

Other aspects of the learner that have an impact on the learning process are displayed in box 5. These factors include

EXHIBIT 4.1
Characteristics of Adult Learners

General physical ability, including health, acuity of senses, special abilities and limitations, and reaction time.
Preferences for using sensory perceptions.
Developmental stage and tasks (life, career, and other).
Ability to cope with transitions (life, career, and other).
Motivational orientation to learning.
Motivational strength for learning.
Quality of experiences with education, educational institutions, and learning in general.
Learning and cognitive style.
Feelings, attitudes, and values regarding learning and the specific learning activity being planned.
Intellectual abilities.
Cultural, ethnic, and religious values and norms.
Life role-harmony or role-conflict (such as family, career, civic).
Ability and preference for working alone or with others.
Study habits, learning strategies, and test anxiety.
Need for support, direction, and structure.
Life, work, and other experiences.
Communication (verbal, written, and psychomotor skills).
Persistence.
Preferences for conditions for learning (such as amount of sound, light, temperature, room design, time of day, mobility, and food intake).
Need for food, water, shelter, physical safety, social acceptance, and personal growth.

physiological abilities and limitations (such as general health, acuity of sensory perceptions, special abilities, and reaction time); developmental stages and experience with life transitions; role conflict or harmony in the person's life; affective factors (such as feelings and emotions); personal values and attitudes

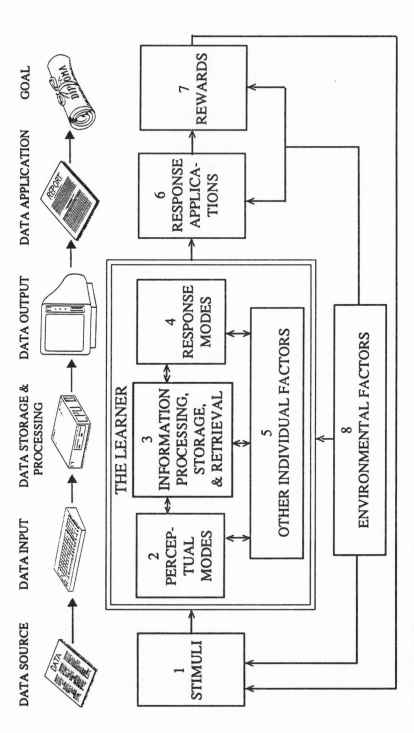

Figure 4.1 The Learning Process: A Computer Analogy
Adapted from: Dean and Kalamas (1987)

regarding learning; motivational orientation and strength of motivation for learning; persistence; prior experience in educational settings and with learning in general; prior experience with the specific content or topics being learned; intellectual abilities; cultural, ethnic, and religious values and norms; ability and preference for working alone or with others; study habits and skills; need for support, direction, and structure in the learning setting; life, work, and other experiences; and preferences for the physical conditions in the learning setting.

Applications of learners' responses are identified in box 6, and include recalling information acquired, solving problems, displaying attitudes or values, or demonstrating psychomotor skills. Each application corresponds to learning outcomes (i.e., domains of learning, discussed in Chapter 7) and is directed at achieving some reward or goal for the learner (box 7). Examples of rewards and goals to which learners might respond include getting a job, receiving a good grade, acquiring a diploma or certificate, improving their self-esteem, or expanding their knowledge and horizons. The computer analogy is somewhat incongruous with reality at this point. The rewards are depicted as external to the learner, but their salience and meaning are internal. Box 7 is separated from the main figure to emphasize the importance of goals in the learning process.

Environmental factors affecting learning are shown in box 8. These include the cultural context, organizational and community climate, structure of the educational program in which the learner is engaged, the learning setting (both physical and psychological) created by the adult educator, and institutional, informational, and situational barriers which the learner faces.

Stimuli flows from the first box to the learner (boxes 2, 3, 4, and 5). Learning represented in the boxes is interactive; any part of the process potentially affects any other. Responses flow from the learner to a specific application (box 6) to achieve a specific reward (box 7). All factors—the stimuli, the learner, the response applications, and the rewards—occur in and are affected by environmental factors (box 8). Last, feedback from the response applications and goals of the learner affects the activities of the adult educator structuring the activity.

This computer analogy has some limitations. People are more complicated than computers. "Garbage in, garbage out" is true of computers, but people are selective about the stimuli they acquire and how they use them—they can make sense out of incomplete information or misconstrue the clearest of instructions. People have selective memories, are able to prioritize information, and can relate new information to old. Most important, people are not passive like computers but are capable of initiating learning.

Nevertheless, the factors that affect learning and the relationships among those factors can be identified through the computer analogy. Using a computer analogy makes it possible to understand the processes of acquiring and using information in the context of a systems approach. The systems approach helps to identify events or series of events which occur during learning as well as factors which affect the learning process. It also helps the adult educator determine which learner characteristics are relevant, possible to assess, and have the most meaning for a particular learning situation.

SUMMARY

Chapter 4 focused on defining learners' needs and motivations and identifying characteristics of learners which can be assessed. Learning needs are internally or externally identified discrepancies between an ideal and real state, and motivation is the force that drives a learner to participate in learning to reduce that discrepancy. Motivation to participate is sometimes stymied by barriers either internal to the person or resident in the learning program, community, or society.

Figure 4.1, The Learning Process: A Computer Analogy, helps the adult educator understand the factors which may be of value to assess and to identify the relationships among those factors.

In the next chapter, strategies for assessing various learner characteristics identified in this chapter are addressed to present options for adult educators to consider.

CHAPTER 5

Learner Needs Assessment Strategies

In instructional design, needs assessment usually implies a data gathering and interpretation process through which learner needs and characteristics are identified, assessed, and used to develop learning activities and materials. A basic premise of this book is that needs assessment is a broader concept that may be applied to a number of areas including assessing your own strengths and weaknesses as an adult educator and assessing the learning content and contexts, in addition to assessing the learners. In this chapter, however, needs assessment in its traditional sense of assessing the characteristics of learners is considered.

Why is it important to assess learner needs? The obvious answer is that an educator requires certain information to develop learning activities that are appropriate for the learners. Needs assessment, however, can be used for other purposes as well. From a program planning perspective, for instance, conducting needs assessment is a useful way to publicize a program, provide public relations, and create linkages with other organizations. In addition, needs assessment can contribute to learner commitment to current and future educational programs.

How can I learn all I need to know about my adult learners? The ways and means for collecting data about, by, and from adult learners are many. This chapter explores in some detail strategies for conducting learner needs assessment. Discussion of planning assessment and strategies for assessing are followed by sampling strategies and developing needs assessment reports.

PLANNING LEARNER NEEDS ASSESSMENT

Who should be included in learner needs assessment and when should it be done? It is important to decide in advance who is going to help make decisions, gather and interpret the data, and when these activities are to take place. Then, three conditions are necessary to determine the extent to which educational needs exist: (1) an accurate assessment of the current state of the learner's knowledge, attitudes, or skills; (2) a clear understanding and agreement on the desired state of the learner's knowledge, attitudes, or skills; and (3) an understanding and agreement that any differences observed can, in fact, be diminished or eliminated through education. The potential relationships between the learners, the adult education provider, and the timing of the needs assessments are described in Figure 5.1, Planning Learner Needs Assessment.

Vertical columns in Figure 5.1 indicate the timing of the needs assessment. Horizontal rows indicate who has primary responsibility for conducting the needs assessment. In cell 1, the adult educator is responsible for conducting the needs assessment prior to the learning activity. In this case, the adult educator identifies the relevant characteristics of the learners and develops a means of assessing those characteristics prior to the beginning of the course or workshop. Options for carrying out prior assessment include surveys, pretests, observation, assessment centers, or interviews. In this approach the adult educator is responsible for establishing the goals and objectives of the learning activity; learner input is secondary, if considered at all.

Needs assessment conducted during the learning activity by the adult educator is represented in cell 2. Techniques used at the beginning of and during the learning activity can be formal, such as surveys and tests, or informal, such as observation and interviews with the learners. The adult educator "reads" the learners and makes decisions to fine-tune activities.

Cell 3 represents a collaborative effort between the educator and learners to assess needs before the learning takes place through Delphi or Nominal Group Technique, quality circles,

TIMING OF THE NEEDS ASSESSMENT

		Before the Learning Activity	During the Learning Activity
WHO CONDUCTS THE NEEDS ASSESSMENT	Adult Educator	☐ Surveys ☐ Pretests ☐ Observation ☐ Assessment Centers ☐ Interviews	☐ Surveys ☐ Tests ☐ Observation ☐ Interviews
	Collaborative	☐ Delphi ☐ Nominal Group Technique ☐ Quality Circles ☐ Discussion Groups ☐ Learning Contracts	☐ Discussion Groups ☐ Modifications of Learning Contracts ☐ Nominal Group Technique
	Learners	☐ Citizen Groups ☐ Task Forces ☐ Quality Circles ☐ Self-Identification of Felt or Expressed Needs ☐ Self-Directed Learner	☐ Continuous Self-Monitoring ☐ Development of Self-Directed Learning

Figure 5.1 Planning Learner Needs Assessment

discussion groups, learning contracts, or other methods which bring the adult educator and the learners together to plan the learning activity. This approach implies shared responsibility for developing instructional goals and objectives.

Learners and adult educators also can collaborate to assess needs during the learning activity, as depicted in cell 4. Methods used to assess learning needs during the learning activity include discussion groups, modifications of learning contracts, and the use of Nominal Group Technique.

In cell 5, the learners are responsible for conducting their own needs assessment prior to the learning activity. This could be necessary in the case of citizen groups requesting services from an educational institution, or employees identifying a need for new learning and presenting their needs to management. Learners might express their needs in these situations through task forces, quality circles, and self-identification of felt needs. Individual self-directed learners, too, might determine learning needs on their own.

Cell 6 represents the situation in which learners come to the adult educator during the course of a program and state their needs. If the facilitator has created an open and trusting atmosphere, then learners may feel free to present their needs to the facilitator as they develop. The needs of adult learners are not static; they cannot be assessed once and then dismissed. Needs assessment is ongoing and involves constant adjustments in course material, methods, climate, and relationships. As the adult learners grow and develop, they may be able to identify new needs not previously anticipated.

Having decided who will conduct the assessment and when it will be conducted, the next major decisions are what characteristics to assess and how to assess them. Being selective about the characteristics which should be assessed is essential. Frequently, the educator must make compromises between what is desirable to know about the learners and what is feasible given cost, time, expertise required, and the degree to which learners are willing and able to undergo various forms of assessment.

STRATEGIES FOR COLLECTING
NEEDS ASSESSMENT DATA

In general, there are four ways to obtain information about learners: (1) through one's own personal and professional experience, (2) consulting others who are knowledgeable about the learners, (3) conducting a review of the literature, and (4) direct data gathering techniques (Dean & Ferro, 1991).

Personal and Professional Experience

Personal experience is a reasonable place to begin the process of needs assessment. What was learned from your experiences with these or similar groups of learners? What experience and skills do they bring with them into the learning situation? What needs (personal and professional) do they have? And, perhaps most important, how far can you trust your own judgment on these issues, and when do you need to bring in other forms of needs assessment? A framework for analyzing your personal and professional experience is provided in Activity 5.1, Using Personal and Professional Experience for Needs Assessment. This activity emphasizes that you can rely on your experience to answer some but not all questions you might have about your learners. It is important to realize that you cannot assume that you know everything there is to know about particular learners based on your past experience with similar people.

Experts

Consulting other knowledgeable people is often an expeditious way of obtaining information about learners and can be accomplished informally through personal contacts or formally through structured techniques such as Delphi or Nominal Group Technique. The experts can be supervisors, key people in an or-

---

ACTIVITY 5.1
Using Personal and Professional
Experience for Needs Assessment*

A. What does my personal experience tell me about:

1. the context and setting of the program?
2. what the learners already know?
3. what the learners need to learn?

B. What do I need to find out about:

1. the context and the setting?
2. the prospective learners?
3. the content and topic to be learned?

*Adapted from Dean and Ferro (1991).

---

ganization or community, or those who have studied the learners, the community, or the organization.

The primary danger in consulting other people is the limitations of their views. If you consult just a few experts and rely heavily on their judgment about the learners, you may end up with the opinions of a few isolated people who may be biased or not as well informed as you thought. It is best to acquire information from many "experts" for a variety of perspectives and experience.

Literature Reviews

Using the professional literature is one of the best ways of finding out what is known about adult learners. There are many sources of information to consult. Literature can be selected from adult education, K–12 education, psychology, sociology, business, counseling, and a number of other fields to provide background information about certain characteristics of different groups of adult learners. More specifically, literature searches can be conducted using ERIC (Educational Resources Information Clearinghouse), PsychInfo (journal articles and resources in psychology), Sociological Abstracts, and Dissertation Abstracts International. These are just a few of the many data bases available for literature searches.

Perhaps the biggest drawback of using existing literature for a needs assessment is finding information that can be applied to your specific group of learners. In many, if not most, cases existing literature will be of general interest, informing you about more general characteristics of learners rather than specific characteristics of a specific group of participants in a program.

Getting started conducting literature reviews can be a daunting task, especially for someone not used to using modern research library resources. Merriam and Simpson (2000) provide an excellent resource for conducting literature reviews in *A Guide to Research for Educators and Trainers of Adults.*

Direct Data Gathering Techniques

The fourth method of learning about your learners is direct data gathering techniques. There are many ways to elicit information from learners, but the five techniques that appear to be useful to most adult educators are interviews, discussion groups, observation, commercially available instruments, and locally constructed instruments.

Interviews

Interviews most easily allow the educator to broach sensitive issues and elicit subtle or complex responses, but conducting interviews and analyzing the data are time consuming. Often only a small number of learners can be interviewed so it is important to select the interviewees carefully. Real dangers in this process are selecting only those who will give favorable responses or paying attention only to those who are most outspoken in their criticism.

Interviews can be tailored to fit different purposes. Conducting a structured interview is like conducting an oral survey: predetermined questions or items are presented to learners orally for their responses. During unstructured or semistructured interviews, learners are asked open-ended questions which call for their opinions or perspectives. This allows the interviewer to focus on issues the learner identifies as important and to pursue ideas as they occur. It is important to maintain an appropriate level of structure: too much structure may put words in the learner's mouth or result in inadequately expressed views, but too little structure may result in unfocused or irrelevant responses. Guidelines for developing an effective semistructured interview are listed in Exhibit 5.1. Conducting effective interviews is explored more fully in Guba and Lincoln (1982), Krueger (1997), and Vaughn, Schumm, and Sinagub (1996).

Groups

Using group techniques for needs assessment is a favorite strategy of adult educators. Both highly structured techniques such as Nominal Group, Delphi, and Participation Training, and less structured techniques such as focus groups, brainstorming, buzz groups, and general discussion groups are useful.

In Nominal Group Technique opinions can be ascertained and prioritized to form a list. The technique takes only 2 to 4 hours, and it is most effective with 10 to 20 participants. The process is further described in Korhonen (1998) and Delbecq, Van de Ven, and Gustafson (1975).

Delphi groups accomplish the same purpose as Nominal groups but are used when the participants are scattered geographically and cannot be pulled together in one location; completion may take several weeks or months, although the use of e-mail or chat functions can greatly expedite the process. One or more questions are sent to members of the Delphi panel, and their responses are synthesized and returned for further comment. This process is repeated until consensus or clear trends in the data are observed. The Delphi technique is described in more detail in Delbecq, Van de Ven, and Gustafson (1975).

EXHIBIT 5.1
Guidelines for Developing
an Effective Semistructured Interview

1. Determine the concepts to be addressed—form preliminary ideas on the makeup (number and proportion of topics) and boundaries of the interviews.

2. Develop open-ended questions which address your main points (keeping in mind the topics, their proportion, and the boundaries you have already established).

3. Do not use questions that can be answered "yes or no" or by any other one-word answers—you want people to talk about what they feel, believe, have done, will do, like, dislike, etc. Try starting questions with "Tell me about . . . "; "What do you think about . . . "; "How did that make you feel . . . "; "If you could do it over again, what would you do?"

4. Field test your interview questions with people who are like the ones you intend to interview.

5. Contact the prospective interviewees by phone or by mail. Let them know how you got their name. Explain the purpose of your study clearly and early in the conversation. If you plan to tape the interviews, tell the person this up-front. Send a consent form in advance of the interview if possible, and if not, give it to the person to sign before the interview begins.

6. Start the interview with easy or nonthreatening questions. Allow time to build rapport with the participant before you get into more difficult or sensitive issues.

7. Establish a positive pattern at the beginning of the interview. Put the person at ease. Let the interviewee do most of the talking—you are there to listen and learn, not lecture.

8. Use prompters if the interviewee does not respond to your initial questions. Start with the most general questions—the

ones which lead the least, then use more specific questions as needed to prompt a response. For example, the following questions are arranged from most general to the more specific: (1) "I noticed that you did not complete school . . . " (2) "What were you feeling when you dropped out of school?" (3) "What was happening in school or in your personal life when you quit school?" (4) "Can you name some things which may have influenced your decision to quit school?"

9. Bring the interview to a close. Summarize the main points and reiterate why you are doing the interview. Let the interviewee know that you are available if there are questions.

There are several different variations of discussion groups used in adult education, some more structured than others. Skills required to run successful discussion groups are described by Brookfield (1998). Specific group processes, such as buzz sessions and brainstorming, are discussed in Bergevin, Morris, and Smith (1963) and Seaman (1977).

Observation

Observations can be formal or informal. Informal observation is an extensively used assessment technique. Many adult educators observe their learners and deduce from their observations what the learners need to do to be successful. The problem with informal observation is that the observers' biases are not necessarily taken into consideration. Is the observer seeing what is actually occurring with the learners or only seeing what he or she wants to see? Informal observations can be made on the job, in the community, or in other settings. For example, a trainer may spend time with employees on their jobs to get a better understanding of their work activities.

Formal observations can occur in a variety of settings including simulation and role-play activities, assessment centers, and supervisors' reports and evaluations, and are often presented as written case studies or profiles of learners' potential abilities and skills. Checklists and time-motion studies are some of the strategies for observation discussed in Guba and Lincoln (1982).

Standardized Assessment Instruments

There are literally thousands of commercially prepared standardized instruments available to assess learner needs and characteristics. The best source of information on standardized instruments is the *Buros Institute of Mental Measures* (1938–2001), published by the Buros Institute, University of Nebraska, Lincoln. These books are available at most academic libraries in the reference section. There are many criteria for judging the value of a standardized test, some of the more important are addressed in Exhibit 5.2, Selecting Standardized Assessment Instruments for Assessing Learner Needs and Characteristics. When selecting a standardized instrument there are three critical questions to ask yourself. First, is the purpose of the instrument appropriate? This is really three questions: is the instrument appropriate for the learners, is it appropriate for the organization in which you work, and is it appropriate for you as the adult educator? Second, are the psychometrics of the instrument sound? This question addresses the technical aspects of validity and reliability. Third, are the results of the instrument useful for the purpose for which you intend to use them? The issues raised by these questions are explored more completely in Exhibit 5.2.

Locally Constructed Instruments and Procedures

Locally constructed instruments can be designed to assess knowledge, attitudes, and skills. Often these instruments are used to identify specific needs or characteristics for which commercial instruments are not available. Factors to consider when constructing instruments locally are purpose (characteristics to be assessed); sophistication of the learners (their experience with

---

EXHIBIT 5.2
Selecting Standardized Assessment Instruments
for Assessing Learner Needs and Characteristics

The following questions may help you compare and contrast various instruments to determine which would be most useful for your purposes.

1. What is the purpose of the instrument? Is this appropriate for the learners?

2. With what groups have norms been established for the instrument? Are these groups similar to the learners you intend to assess?

3. How much does it cost? Can you afford it?

4. How much time does it take to administer? Is this realistic?

5. Does the instrument require special expertise to administer, score, or interpret? If so, can you acquire the expertise?

6. Can learners and adult educators readily use the information provided by the instrument? Do the results answer the questions you and the learners have?

7. Are the format and reading level of the instrument appropriate for the learners?

8. Are the validity and reliability of the instrument sufficient for your purposes?

9. Can the instrument be hand scored? Does machine scoring cost extra? Will there be a time delay in having the instrument sent to the publisher for machine scoring?

---

and skill in completing assessment instruments); costs and logistics of distributing, administering, collecting, and analyzing the data; and the type of information it will yield.

Answering the following questions can help in developing a needs assessment instrument: (1) What is important to find out about the learners? (2) What types of questions will help get that information? (3) How can the questions be phrased? (4) For what purposes is the information going to be used (in what form should the information appear at the end)? Types of items which can be used in locally constructed needs assessment instruments are identified, with their purposes, in Exhibit 5.3.

Locally constructed instruments can be employed on-site, directly before or during a learning experience, as in the case of pretests. They can also be used well in advance of the learning experience, as in the case of surveys. Because surveys are often used, they are discussed in detail in the next section.

Surveys

A survey is a common method for needs assessment in adult education when large numbers of adult learners are involved. The first step in conducting surveys for needs assessments is to clearly identify the purpose of the survey by answering the following questions: what data should be collected, from whom should the data be collected, what decisions will be made with the data, how will the data be analyzed, how will the data be reported, and to whom will the data be reported? The answers to these questions will guide the educator in developing the instrument and selecting a sample.

There are two aspects to developing a survey instrument: selecting the types of items to be used on the instrument, and designing the overall format and appearance of the instrument. The information in Exhibit 5.3 can help in this process. Items should be selected with care to elicit the right kind of information, and to be appropriate for the adult learners expected to respond to them. Additional help for developing questionnaire items and formatting the questionnaire can be obtained from Sudman and Bradburn (1987) and Schumin and Presser (1996).

EXHIBIT 5.3
Types of Questions for Locally Constructed
Learner Needs Assessment Instruments

1. **Select One:** Respondents are instructed to select one response from a list. This is used for items in which only one response is desired. Each response must be mutually exclusive, that is, respondents cannot be able to select more than one response. Also, all possible responses must be anticipated or an "Other" response must be included. Examples:

   a. Gender (circle one):   Male   Female

   b. Employment status   Employed full time
      (circle one):   Employed part time
                       Not employed

   c. I am a graduate student   Yes   No
      (circle one):

   d. Educational status   _____ Less than 12th grade
      (check one):   _____ High school graduate
                      _____ Some college
                      _____ Associate's degree
                      _____ Bachelor's degree
                      _____ Some graduate school
                      _____ Master's degree
                      _____ Doctoral degree
                      _____ Other: _____

2. **Fill in the Blank:** Respondents are instructed to complete a sentence or phrase by supplying the missing information. This is used to solicit information that may have too many different responses for each to be listed. It must be clear what information is requested. In the first example, it is relatively clear that the respondent is to write their chronological age. In the second example it is not clear if the respondent is to list years of education, degrees, or some other response. Examples:

a. Age: _____
b. Highest level of education: _____

3. **Rating Scale:** Respondents are instructed to rate an item by selecting a number on a scale. This is used to ascertain the opinions, feelings, beliefs, and attitudes of respondents on selected issues. Scaled items provide richer data than Select One or Check List items and are therefore preferable. The key to good scaled items is to have clear descriptors (anchor points). Also, you need to decide if you want an even number of points on the scale (which keeps people from selecting the middle) or an odd number of points. Usually it is best to have between 4 and 7 points on the scale. This gives sufficient range for the scores to be spread out without giving the respondent too many choices. Examples:

   a. (Agreement): Enrolling in adult education is the best thing I ever did.

Strongly Disagree	Disagree	Not Sure	Agree	Strongly Agree
1	2	3	4	5

   b. (Frequency): I have my assignments done on time:

Never	Seldom	Sometimes	Frequently	Always
1	2	3	4	5

   c. (Amount): I like to do research:

Not at All	A Little	Somewhat	A Lot	A Great Deal
1	2	3	4	5

   d. (Importance): To me, getting good grades is:

Not at All Important	Very Little Importance	Somewhat Important	Important	Very Important
1	2	3	4	5

4. **Rank Order:** Respondents are instructed to rank a list in order of preference or some other criteria. This is primarily used to identify priorities of respondents. It is important that all responses are applicable to each respondent so that they can be ranked. Examples:

    a. Rank order the following list from 1 to 6 with 1 = least important activity for a manager and 6 = most important activity for a manager.

        _____ Writing effective reports

        _____ Making effective presentations

        _____ Handling employee discipline problems

        _____ Motivating employees

        _____ Developing employee learning teams

        _____ Managing time

5. **Check List:** Respondents are instructed to select the responses that apply to them from a list. Respondents may select none, some, or all of the responses from the list. This is primarily used to allow respondents to identify their preferences, desires, use of services, etc. Each response must be treated as a separate item for data analysis. Examples:

    a. From the following list, select topics you would like to see offered as elective courses (check all that appeal to you):

        _____ Distance education

        _____ Preparing budgets for adult education programs

        _____ Critical theory in adult education

        _____ International adult education

        _____ Advanced statistical analysis

        _____ Other: _____

6. **Multiple Choice:** Respondents are asked to select one correct response from several choices. This is primarily used for testing knowledge or understanding of concepts. There are two major cautions regarding using multiple choice items. First, there must one "right" answer to each question. Second, good multiple choice items are difficult to write. Considerable research goes into the development of "item pools" for national, normed tests using multiple choice items. Examples:

a. The 1989 *Handbook of Adult and Continuing Education* was edited by:
   a. Darkenwald and Merriam
   b. Merriam and Cunningham
   c. Brookfield and Meziorw
   d. Dean and Ferro

7. **True-False:** Respondents are instructed to identify if a statement is "true" or "false." This is primarily used for testing knowledge or understanding of concepts. There are three major cautions regarding using true-false items. First, there must be a "right" answer to each item. Second, good true-false items are difficult to write. Third, the respondent has a 50% chance of guessing the correct answer. Examples:

   a. Malcolm Knowles coined the term *andragogy*.
      True   False

8. **Open-Ended:** Respondents are asked to write a response in which their options are not limited. This is used to allow respondents to discuss issues not addressed in closed-ended items on a survey. It also allows respondents to express their opinions about issues. Open-ended items are used when all of the concerns of the respondents cannot be addressed through the closed-ended items. Examples:

   a. What are the most important issues facing the field of adult education today?
   b. The goals of this organization in the next year should be:

Steps for developing the survey questionnaire itself are identified in Exhibit 5.4, Guidelines for Developing Survey Questionnaires.

Next, the educator must select a sample to survey. It may not be necessary to obtain information from all potential or actual learners to make general decisions about content, format, and structure of the learning situation. In fact, a sample of the learners may better serve your purposes. If information about specific experiences or skills of the adult learners is needed, then it will be necessary to assess all learners.

EXHIBIT 5.4
Guidelines for Developing Survey Questionnaires

---

1. Make the layout attractive; use white space appropriately on the paper.

2. Make the directions easy to read and follow.

3. Place the title, the purpose, and the directions on the first page so that respondents can refer to them.

4. Arrange the items in a logical order. Items can be ordered in the following ways:

   Easy to hard items—hard items are the more sensitive or difficult to complete.

   Chronological order—if your items relate to activities which have time sequence.

   Item type—for example, all true-false, then all multiple choice, then all continuum items, etc.

   Topic—arrange the items in groups according to the topics addressed.

5. All pages on the survey should be numbered consecutively—do not have sections with numbers starting over.

6. Repeat the directions and/or the scale for item completion at the top of each new page—do not assume that respondents will remember what they are supposed to do.

7. Place directions at each place where there is a change in the questionnaire (change of format, change of items, etc.)

8. Keep continuum items parallel—unless there is a good reason to change the format. For example, if a scale of "1 to 5" is used, the items should all be written so that "5" is the most positive response and "1" is the most negative response. This will aid in data analysis and interpretation.

9. Number all items one through x—do not start numbering over or have sections if possible. This will be a major aid in data analysis.

10. Do not ask more than one question per item.

11. Have several people read your questionnaire for clarity of directions, ease of completion, appearance, typos, and content before you mail it out.

12. Remember—if it can be misunderstood, it will be misunderstood!

Sampling is a complex business, but several guidelines can be used to simplify the task. First, determine the number of potential learners. Second, determine if sampling is needed or if you can and should assess all of the learners by weighing the number of learners against how much time and money you have, the extent of the needs assessment required for each learner, the time and expertise needed to interpret the data, and whether it is necessary to give each learner individual feedback from the needs assessment. If sampling rather than a comprehensive needs assessment is indicated, choose a sampling method such as random sampling, stratified random sampling, cluster sampling, or purposeful sampling. More thorough discussions on sampling strategies can be found in Babbie (1973) and Gay (2000).

In random sampling, a sample of learners is selected from a population by using a table of random numbers or other suitable method. The number needed for a sample will vary depending upon the size of the total pool of learners, the time and money available for the needs assessment, and the degree of accuracy desired of the findings. The larger the sample, the more likely the findings will represent the whole pool or population of learners.

Stratified random sampling can be used when the pool of learners should be divided into groups (for example, learners from different geographic areas or different levels of preparation). The educator must (1) determine the groups or categories of learners to be surveyed, (2) acquire a list of learners in each group or category, (3) select a certain number of learners from each group or category, and (4) collect the desired information from each group or category. In stratified random sampling, a random sample is drawn from each group or category which has been identified.

If the learners are already enrolled in one or more institutions or classes, it may be possible to randomly select some of the institutions or classes of learners for the needs assessment. This is known as cluster sampling. In this case a complete list of classes is needed as well as a complete list of the learners enrolled in each class. Rather than selecting individuals, classes are selected randomly for data collection.

Selecting learners because they possess certain characteristics (for example, the best students in a program or those exhibiting certain attitudes, values, or beliefs) is called purposeful sampling. Often, this is the method used with interviewing since interviewing is so time intensive. When purposeful sampling is conducted, be sure that a thorough rationale is developed to determine who is to be included in the sample.

ANALYZING AND REPORTING NEEDS ASSESSMENT DATA

As mentioned at the beginning of the chapter, there are a number of reasons for conducting needs assessment including learning about the learners, developing publicity and public relations, securing funding, creating agency linkages, and building learner commitment. These considerations influence the type of data which is collected as well as how it is analyzed and reported.

Decisions made regarding analyzing and reporting needs assessment data should be made prior to collecting it. Questions which should be asked to determine the method of the analysis and reporting include (1) Why and when were the data collected? (2) Under what conditions or by what methods were the data collected? (3) Who is responsible for analyzing and reporting the data? (4) What methods will be used to analyze the data? (5) How will the data be reported? and (6) To whom will the data be reported?

Analyzing the Data

In Exhibit 5.3, several different types of questions which can be used for learner needs assessment are shown. Each type of question results in different types of data. Checklist items provide nominal data from which frequencies and percentages can be computed. These can be summarized in bar or pie graphs to allow for easy comparisons. Ranking items result in ordinal data which can be analyzed using median scores. The medians can be computed for each item, for the whole group of respondents, or for various subgroups if desired. In some situations, group responses can be compared using chi-square or nonparametric analysis.

Rating scale and multiple choice questions result in interval or ratio data which allows for the computation of frequencies, percents, means, and standard deviations for individuals or groups. The data can be useful for determining the level of knowledge or proficiency in a content domain. They can be analyzed using t-tests, analysis of variance, multiple regression, and other more sophisticated analyses.

Open-ended questions are often more problematic to analyze. A useful method is referred to as content analysis. Through this method all of the responses are analyzed and the themes or recurring comments that can be used to identify the thoughts of the respondents on the important issues are identified.

Large amounts of numerical data almost demand the use of computers for storage, management, and analysis. Statistical software packages are available for both mainframe computers and for microcomputers. Computers and statistical software are recommended because of the speed and accuracy of analysis and the variety of options available for analysis.

Reporting the Data

The intended audience determines how the data are reported. Data presentation for the public is offered in different forms than that used to help secure funding for programs. Usually needs assessments conducted on a large scale will involve detailed technical reports which consist of several sections or chapters. The common sections are (1) a statement of the purpose of the needs assessment study; (2) a review of the methodology involved in the study, including the method of sampling and data collection and analysis processes; (3) a presentation of the findings of the study, and (4) a discussion of the uses of the findings. Often these reports are prefaced with an executive summary—a three-to-five page synopsis of the report. Technical reports are used for funding sources, dissemination to other agencies and organizations, and publication in professional journals or ERIC (Educational Resources Information Clearinghouse).

Shorter and less detailed reports are often used for internal institutional purposes. These often take the same general form as a full technical report, but include fewer details. Also, the methodology section may be abbreviated or eliminated if the procedures used are known and understood by the audience.

Dissemination of information to the public usually calls for reporting only the highlights from the findings through pamphlets, newsletters, news releases, and other popular formats. Releasing this type of information may help publicize program activities. A real danger of releasing abbreviated needs analysis data, however, is misinterpretation by the public because the complexity of the data collection and analysis process may not be fully understood. The adult educator assumes responsibility for accurately reporting needs assessment data.

SUMMARY

Learner needs assessment can be very complex or straight-forward, but time spent thinking through the issues of learner needs assessment will be well worthwhile. The issues to be considered for needs assessment are identifying the following:

1. Learner characteristics to be assessed

2. Assignment of responsibility for conducting the needs assessment

3. Timing and number of needs assessments

4. Involvement of learners in developing, conducting, and interpreting the needs assessment

5. Techniques used to assess the learners

6. Sampling strategy to be used

7. Method of analyzing and reporting the data

8. Ways the needs assessment data can be used to individualize instruction for the learners

Learner needs are but one of four areas requiring assessment prior to curriculum development. The other three areas are assessment of yourself as an adult educator, assessment of content to be learned, and assessment of contexts in which the learning takes place. Context assessment is the subject of the next chapter.

CHAPTER 6

Understanding the Learning Contexts

In the opening scene of *The Music Man* several traveling salesmen are on a train heading through the Midwest. The more experienced salesman is heard intoning this advice to the neophyte: "You gotta know the territory!" So does the adult educator. The "territory" is the context in which the instructional plan is developed and implemented. In this chapter, our attention is directed to two issues related to the learning contexts: defining and assessing the context.

DEFINING THE CONTEXTS

The context is the surrounding social, political, economic, and other forces that impact on the instructional design process and the teaching-learning transaction. Most adult education is sponsored by or involved in some way with formal organizations. Formal organizations are the "social structures created by individuals to support the collaborative pursuit of specific goals" (Scott, 1981, p. 9). Examples of organizations in which adult education programs commonly exist include educational institutions, businesses, hospitals, community service agencies, governmental agencies, prisons, churches, libraries, and museums. These organizations, in turn, exist in a context of their own—an extended context or community. The community can be defined by geographical proximity, for example, neighborhoods or school districts (Brookfield, 1983), or as a group of people with a common identity (Dean & Dowling, 1987).

Several levels of contexts can usually be identified depending on the complexity of the learning situation. The first level is the person or group of people providing the adult education activities; in large organizations with departments devoted to adult education, the department itself is another level of context which must often be taken into account. The next level of context is the sponsoring organization in which the adult education activities occur. A still larger level of context is the environment surrounding the parent organization. For example, in a human resource development department providing training in business and industry, the context may be defined first as the training department, second as the organization in which the training is taking place, and third as the community in which the organization resides. Directors of community education for school districts or hospitals, however, would define the context first as the department in which they work, second as the school system or hospital, and third as the communities served by the school or agency. Examples of learning contexts are depicted in Figure 6.1, Sample Learning Contexts.

Much has been written about the relationship between adult education providers and their sponsoring organizations. According to Schroeder (1970), adult education providers reside in one of four organizational settings: (1) institutions devoted primarily to adult education, (2) institutions devoted primarily to youth education in which adult education is a secondary function, (3) adult education as a complementary function of a quasi-educational institution, and (4) adult education as a secondary or supportive function of a noneducational institution. Institutions devoted primarily to adult education may have only one level of context within the organization. Other organizations will usually have at least two levels o contexts—more if the organization is very large or complex.

The nature of an organization gives clues to understanding how the contexts will affect adult education programs and the learning activities. Scott (1981) described three perspectives, the rational, natural, and open systems, that can be used to understand how organizations work. The rational systems perspective was fueled by the industrial revolution, the assembly line, and more recently, plant automation. Specialization of jobs and pre-

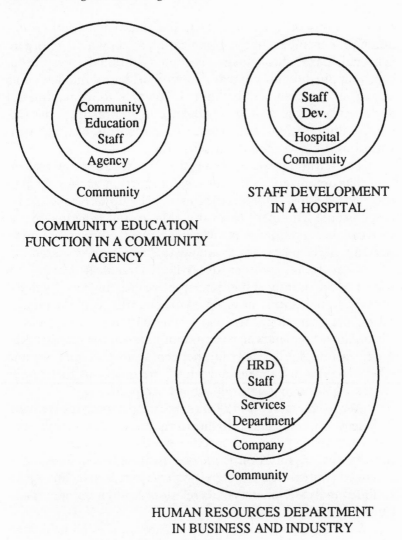

COMMUNITY EDUCATION
FUNCTION IN A COMMUNITY
AGENCY

STAFF DEVELOPMENT
IN A HOSPITAL

HUMAN RESOURCES DEPARTMENT
IN BUSINESS AND INDUSTRY

Figure 6.1 Sample Learning Contexts

cise lines of communication in a hierarchical pyramid are the hallmarks of this approach to understanding and managing organizations. An assumption underlying this approach is that organizations could be managed by arranging people according to specific jobs and functions. A rational systems perspective is often demonstrated by line, staff, and functional relationships among the members of the organization as shown on an organizational chart. This system, based on a "rational" perspective, can be applied to any context and will yield a useful view of its structure. The view will be limited, however, to formal lines of authority and responsibility as defined in an organization's formal communications, such as mission statements, charters, constitutions, by-laws, and job descriptions.

The natural systems perspective resulted from the realization that organizations do not always function as they are represented on paper. Organizations are made up of people, and it is the people who make them function, or not function, as the case may be. A natural systems perspective facilitates an understanding of the relationships among the people, their shared values and attitudes, and their differences. Organizational culture is part of the natural systems perspective. Schein (1992) defined organizational culture as made up of the artifacts of the organization (its technology, art, and visible patterns), the values of the organization, and the basic assumptions of the people in the organization. "What is really happening in this context, and who is making it happen, and why?" are questions that can be addressed through a natural systems perspective.

According to Scott (1981) these two perspectives were not sufficient to understand fully how organizations function. As a result the open systems perspective emerged. Through this perspective the organization is viewed as an entity in a larger or extended context. From an open systems perspective, an organization is analyzed in terms of its relationships with other organizations in its environment.

Scott's three perspectives on organizations can help adult educators develop a more thorough understanding of the various levels of contexts affecting the adult education program and learning activities. In addition to identifying the levels of contexts, the adult educator must also identify the important components within each level of context. The steps involved in developing a thorough understanding of the learning contexts include identifying the contexts, the decision makers in the contexts, the contextual culture, and the environment.

Identifying the Learning Contexts

Identifying the contexts involves several steps. First, list all the major organizations and communities that impact on the adult education activities. For HRD (human resources development) specialists, these may include the human resources development department, other departments in the company, the company itself, parent companies, the community in which the company is located, and professional associations such as the American Society for Training and Development. For the community agency employee, the contexts may consist of the agency; sponsoring organizations and funders; municipal, county, state, or federal governments; and appropriate professional associations. Refer to the diagrams in Figure 6.1, Sample Learning Contexts, for examples of how various configurations of contexts can be identified.

Second, identify the mission, purpose, or unifying themes for each organization. Formal organizations such as businesses, hospitals, community agencies, and schools often have a formal mission or vision statement. In communities, which usually do not have formal mission statements, there are often identifying themes or ideas which can be used to describe the community.

Third, answer the following questions: What are the boundaries of the contexts? Are the boundaries immediate and clearly definable as in the case of a business or agency? Or are they more amorphous as in the case of a community? How many levels of contexts are important to consider? Answers to these and similar questions help the educator identify contexts that might affect the instructional design process.

Lauffer's (1978) model for assessing the status of the open systems perspective of adult education providers also can help educators identify learning contexts. Lauffer described the environment of the organization as consisting of the acceptance and task environments. The acceptance environment is the degree to which the adult education provider is accepted by members of the community. The task environment consists of the publics which directly impinge on the ability of the adult education provider to carry out its mission. Lauffer identifies four categories of publics: resource providers, potential collaborators and competitors, regulators, and actual and potential consumers. The first three Lauffer describes as input publics, those from which strategic resources can be acquired. The last is an output public consisting of those who receive the educational products and services of the adult education provider.

Lauffer's model can be used to analyze the current status of the relationships between various publics and the adult education provider. First, identify all publics the adult education provider contacts, and divide these into the four categories of resource providers, collaborators and competitors, regulators, and consumers. (A single organization may fall into more than one category.) Next, determine the nature of the relationships with the various organizations in each category and what, if any, strategies are needed to improve relationships with the various publics. In this way the potential success or failure of any individual educational program or learning activity and the status both of the adult education provider and of each learning activity can be assessed in relationship to the sponsoring organization and the community.

Identifying the Decision Makers in the Contexts

An analysis of the contexts will reveal that several persons or groups have considerable power and can influence the success or failure of any learning activity. Formal organizational charts of the organization and the political and civic leaders in a community are good places to begin identifying these decision makers. Here are questions that may help identify other influential individuals and their potential impact: Who makes decisions in these contexts? How are the decisions made? Who is included or, perhaps more significant, not included in the decision-making process? What lines of communication are accessible? What are the decision makers' attitudes regarding the adult education provider and its learning activities? Do the decision makers support the programs? If so, why? If not, why not? What will affect the opinions and attitudes of the decision makers? How can the attitudes of the decision makers be bolstered or changed as needed? Often it may appear as though the decision makers are too remote to be interested in a single training program or adult education class, but, in the long run, it usually pays to cultivate positive relationships with them.

Identifying the Contextual Culture

Contextual culture consists of the attitudes, beliefs, and values that are pervasive in the context. These are usually unstated and do not appear in formal organization charters and mission statements, but often represent the unofficial policy of the organization or rules of the community. As members of organizations and communities we do not often think about or commit this cultural context to paper, but we frequently live by it.

When adult education activities support or reinforce the prevailing culture of the organization or community, it is helpful to make this connection explicit to the decision makers and the members in general. When adult education programs run counter to the prevailing cultural values, it may be helpful to present them in as nonthreatening a manner as possible to minimize resistance to the learning program. In either case, adult educators must be able to determine the status of the educational activities being planned relative to the culture of the organization and the community. Some questions to ask about culture include the following: What are the prevailing attitudes regarding learning in general and the specific learning activity being planned? What cultural factors, values, attitudes, and norms in the context shape attitudes toward and participation in learning activities?

ASSESSING THE LEARNING CONTEXTS

To design instruction effectively, you must think politically —not to plot against others, but to be aware of all of the factors that may affect the adult education provider and its learning activities. Good adult education administrators know almost intuitively how to assess the contexts in which they work. They learn to pick up trends, interpret them, and use the information to their advantage. These same skills can also be developed by the less experienced adult educator.

In Activity 6.1, Assessing the Contexts Affecting Learning, several questions focusing on assessment of decision makers, prevailing cultural influences, and potential resources are posed to help assess the ways in which developing and implementing adult education is affected by contexts. In the activity, two levels of contexts are illustrated: the immediate context, represented by the sponsoring organization, and the larger context, represented by the community. There may be additional contexts depending on the complexity of the parent organization in which the adult education provider resides. In addition, in some cases, the extended community may be divided into more than one context to fully understand the impact of the community on the learning activity. In short, adult educators must know the territory; that is, they must be able to discern the number and relevancy of the contexts to the learning activities they are designing. Cervero and Wilson (1994) describe the process of negotiation that adult educators encounter in program planning in *Planning Responsibly for Adult Education*. Leadership, organizational growth, and other related issues, are discussed more fully in *Enhancing Organizational Effectiveness in Adult and Community Education* by Dean, Murk, and Del Prete (2000). In addition, Galbraith, Sisco, and Gugliemino (1997) describe many aspects of administration and program planning in *Administering Successful Programs for Adults*.

SUMMARY

Assessing the context may at first appear to have more relevance for program planning concerns such as marketing funding than for instructional design. There are, however, direct implications for instructional design in the analysis of the contexts.

ACTIVITY 6.1
Assessing the Contexts Affecting Learning

1. *Status of the Adult Education Program within the Immediate Context (Sponsoring Organization):*

   a. What is the mission and purpose of the sponsoring organization? Within that organization, how widely known and shared is this purpose? How does the adult education function relate to this purpose?

   b. What are the line, staff, and functional relationships in the sponsoring organization (rational systems perspective)? How well do these relationships work? How are decisions made and who makes them? How can the adult education function be promoted?

   c. What are the norms, values, and attitudes of the people in the sponsoring organization (natural systems perspective)? What value is placed on learning in the organization, both in formal settings and informally on the job?

   d. What other groups, departments, or organizations inside the sponsoring organization can be identified which can be cultivated to enhance the adult education function (open systems perspective)?

2. *Status of the Adult Education Program in the Larger Context (Community):*

   a. What is the common identity of the community? How widely shared is it? How does the adult education function relate to this identity?

   b. What lines of authority or responsibility in the community might impact on the adult education provider (rational systems perspective)?

   c. What are the norms, values, and attitudes of the people in the community (natural systems perspective)? What value is placed on learning through both formal and informal education?

d. What other groups or organizations in the community can be cultivated to enhance the adult education function (open systems perspective)?

3. *Status of the Specific Learning Program within the Immediate Context (Sponsoring Organization):*

    a. How does this learning activity enhance or support the mission and purpose of the sponsoring organization?
    b. Do the people in positions of power and responsibility support the learning activity (rational systems perspective)? If so, how can their support be maintained? If not, how can their support be gained?
    c. Does this learning activity match the values, norms, and attitudes of members of the organization? If not, can the learning activity or values be changed (natural systems perspective)?
    d. Have the available resources in the organization been tapped to enhance the success of this learning activity? Can collaborations be established or enhanced to ensure the acceptance of the learning activity (open systems perspective)?

4. *Status of the Specific Learning Program in the Larger Context (Community):*

    a. How does the learning activity relate to the common identity of the community? If it does not, can a connection be established? If it does, can the connection be made more obvious or explicit to the members of the community?
    b. Do the people in positions of power and responsibility support the learning activity (rational systems perspective)? If so, how can their support be maintained? If not, how can their support be gained?
    c. Does this learning activity match the values, norms, and attitudes of members of the community (natural systems perspective)? If not, can the learning activity or the values be changed?

d. Have the available resources in the community been tapped to enhance the success of this learning activity (open systems perspective)? Can collaborations be established or enhanced to ensure the acceptance of the learning activity?

The primary instructional design concerns that can be identified and influenced from context analysis are as follows:

1. Specific people or groups to consult in the process of designing the instructional materials can be identified from the context analysis.

2. The contexts will provide clues as to what should be included as goals and objectives of specific adult education programs.

3. The types of learning activities that are most appropriate for the learners may be suggested by contextual culture.

4. The general format of the program, including the length and overall design, and the availability of equipment and facilities are influenced or sometimes even determined by the context.

5. Methods of instruction to which people are accustomed, and potential resistance to new methods can be identified.

6. The methods of learner evaluation that are required or desired may be suggested by an analysis of the contexts.

7. The criteria for judging the success of the adult education program are determined by the contexts.

This chapter has focused on identifying and assessing the contexts that affect designing instruction. At times the impact of the contexts will appear remote. Other times, decision makers or general opinion will intervene to affect the instructional plan directly. Assessing the contexts is part of the overall assessment process which consists of self-assessment, developing content expertise, learning about the learners, and assessing the contexts. In the next chapter, we will discuss how to focus information gained from these assessments on the process of developing learning goals and objectives.

CHAPTER 7

Developing Goals and Objectives

Goals and objectives for instructional activities are developed based on your self-assessment as an adult educator, your content knowledge, a needs assessment of the learners, and an assessment of the learning contexts. Each of these assessments yields information useful in formulating the goals and objectives for instructional activities. Goals are general statements of desired outcomes of the learning process. Objectives define the outcomes, or end results, of the learning process in more specific terms. The following topics are addressed in this chapter: the outcomes of learning, developing learning goals, developing learning objectives, and sequencing goals and objectives. In addition, an example of how to develop goals and objectives is included in this chapter.

OUTCOMES OF LEARNING

Any discussion of developing goals and objectives must begin with a clear picture of the desired outcomes, or "domains" of the learning process. Gagne, Briggs, and Wager (1988) identified five outcomes of learning: intellectual skills, verbal information, cognitive strategies, attitudes, and motor skills. The intellectual skills outcomes of learning are further subdivided into several categories from least to most complex: discriminations, concrete concepts, rules and defined concepts, higher order rules, and problem solving.

Developing goals and objectives for all of the learning outcomes identified by Gagne, Briggs, and Wager (1988) requires a great deal of precision. It can also be very time consuming. When a great deal of precision in developing instructional objectives is called for, using the system of Gagne, Briggs, and Wager may be more effective than the simplified version suggested here.

Using three outcomes of learning—cognitive, affective, and psychomotor—can greatly simplify the process of developing behavioral objectives. The *cognitive* domain consists of two levels of learning outcomes, acquiring information and applying information to solve problems. The *affective* domain consists of feelings, values, commitment, attitudes, and desires. The *psychomotor* domain consists of physical movements and skills. Using learning domains makes it possible to readily identify the type of learning which should result from the learning experience. The domains, then, provide structure and guidance for writing goals and objectives and developing learning activities. For example, if the desired outcome is for learners to be able to acquire certain information, then the goals, objectives, and learning activities should lead to the learner acquiring the information to be learned. In reality, most learning experiences will result in acquisition of goals and objectives in all three of the learning domains.

DEVELOPING LEARNING GOALS

A learning goal is a general statement of the desired outcomes of the learning experience. Goals are often broad in scope and can be divided into two or more objectives. A goal need not be stated in behavioral terms. In fact, a goal usually describes, in general terms, what the learners should know, feel, or be able to do after the learning experience. Subject matter and desired outcomes, the context of the learning situation, the instructor's strengths and needs, and the learners' needs must be taken into account when educators develop learning goals.

Methods for Developing Goals

A variety of methods can be employed to develop learning goals. These methods are discussed in this section.

Goals Based on Desired Learning Outcomes

One typical and traditional approach prescribed in instructional design for developing learning goals is to identify the desired outcomes or behaviors the learners are expected to exhibit after the learning has occurred. In this case goals are based on the content to be learned. This is readily accomplished when there is specific content or skills to be learned that the learners do not currently possess. The learners are not usually involved in developing goals based on desired outcomes because instructors or other content experts determine that certain knowledge, attitudes, or skills are required. These requirements are often based on a task or content analysis. When learners have not been involved in the decision-making process, it is important to help them identify with and develop a sense of ownership of the goals and the learning process so that they will be committed to achieving the goals.

Goals Based on Licensure/Certification

In many cases, goals are established by certification or licensure tests and requirements. The learners may well be aware of the licensure or certification requirements prior to beginning the training program. Even in this case, it is still important for learners to develop a sense of ownership of the learning goals. One way to accomplish this is to have the learners observe people on the job (job shadowing), which may help them recognize the skills and knowledge applied in everyday situations. Appreciation of the skills required to do a job helps learners see the value of the learning goals, objectives, and activities designed to meet the goals.

Goals Based on the Learning Context

Decision makers or prevailing attitudes and values in the learning context may dictate learning goals. This may result in an internal struggle for the adult educator; goals identified by the decision makers may or may not match the adult educator's perception of learners' needs. Political negotiations may replace rational needs assessment as the means for determining learning goals, and no simple advice can be given for coping with these situations. Adult educators must determine for themselves how far they can compromise—how far they will bend before they break. Disagreement between the adult educator and decision makers does not always mean the decision makers are wrong, however. Their assessment may be the result of a bigger picture of the events surrounding the learning program, or their decisions may be tied to the purse strings and political necessity.

Goals Based on the Instructor's Strengths/Needs

Sometimes development of learning goals is made in relation to adult educators themselves. In these cases, adult educators often make decisions of convenience—identifying goals to match their areas of expertise which lend themselves to teaching methods that are comfortable for them. While one can sometimes get lucky and stumble on the right goals this way, it is not a very systematic way to establish learning goals. On the other hand, when educators are hired for particular skills or expertise, this method of developing learning goals may be used in conjunction with other methods.

Goals Based on Learners' Observed Needs

The method most frequently touted as correct in the adult education literature is to develop learning goals based on the learners' observed learning needs—provided that a systematic assessment of learner needs has been conducted. There are a variety of methods for conducting learner needs assessments, including using your own experience, consulting other experts, conducing literature reviews, and using direct data-gathering techniques. These processes were discussed in detail in Chapter 5.

Goals Based on Learners' Expressed Needs

In some cases, learning goals are based on what learners say they want or need to learn without any systematic attempt to corroborate by others or by observation. This is more often the case in recreational or personal development learning than in learning related to careers or general education development. Learning of this kind usually involves the learners selecting goals (or courses) from a list provided by the instructors or the institution.

Considering the Methods for Developing Goals

As will be readily noted, some methods for identifying learning goals discussed above result in a more systematic and thorough list of goals than others. However, the adult educator does not always have complete control over decisions made regarding goal development; it is not too outlandish to say that rational decision making and understanding are sometimes in short supply in the organizations in which adult educators must work. When this is the situation, which is perhaps more often than not, adult educators must be aware of the factors affecting the development of the learning goals.

The adult educator can use three steps when selecting goals: (1) become aware of the various competing goals as they relate to the content, licensure and certification, the context, the adult educator's strengths and weaknesses, and the learner's observed and expressed needs; (2) weigh the various goals and establish priorities for them; and (3) select goals based on what will best meet the needs of the learners. The instructional design decision-making process implies rational decisions, based on thorough knowledge and understanding of the content, the learners, and the contexts.

DEVELOPING LEARNING OBJECTIVES

Learning objectives are derived from the general goal statements which have been developed. Three types of learning objectives, behavioral, content, and problem centered, are described here. Learning objectives are statements which, for behavioral objectives, describe a specific behavior to be learned; for content objectives, identify specific material to be learned; and for problem-centered objectives, describe a problem which the learner should be able to address. Content and problem-centered objectives are really special cases of behavioral objectives not reduced to discrete behaviors. That is to say, all objectives for learning can ultimately be reduced to specific behaviors if they are subdivided sufficiently and made sufficiently discrete. At times, however, following the reductionist logic of the behaviorist to its ultimate conclusion does not make sense.

Behavioral Objectives

Behavioral objectives are based on the specific behaviors to be learned. Identified by task analysis, discussed in Chapter 3, a certain number of behaviors are identified which need to be mastered in order to learn a certain activity.

Made prominent by Tyler (1950), behavioral objectives have been adapted for use in a wide variety of settings. Perhaps one of the best known proponents of behavioral objectives is Mager (1984), who proposed a simple but effective plan for utilizing them to develop training programs. Mager's system calls for objectives to be written in clear, concise, and unambiguous language. Such language makes clear expectations about what is to be learned, how it is to be learned, with what degree of success it is to be learned, and under what conditions it is to be learned.

Mager identified three components of effective objectives: (1) the terminal behavior, (2) the conditions under which the behavior will be demonstrated, and (3) the criteria of acceptable performance. He further states that not all of these components need to appear in each objective, but, nonetheless, reaffirms that the goal of writing effective objectives is to communicate clearly what is expected of the learner. Objective statements are often begun with the phrase "learners will be able to" (LWBAT). If a specific behavior, condition, and criterion can be added to the LWBAT, then a complete and precise objective will result. For example, where learners are expected to manage small discussion groups of learners, the following objective might be appropriate: "Learners will be able to demonstrate the ability to give directions for a role-playing activity to a group of learners in a training program so that at least 90% of the learners understand the directions the first time they are given." The terminal behavior is the ability to give directions to a group for a role play. The condition for demonstrating the terminal behavior is that the learners are in a training program. The criterion for success is that at least 90% of the learners understand the directions the first time they are given.

Content Objectives

Objectives based on an identified amount of material to be learned, rather than specific behaviors, are content objectives. Content objectives can be stated in behavioral terms (based on a learning task analysis), but it is usually unnecessary to do so.

Content objectives are derived by conducting a content analysis of the topics to be learned, discussed in greater detail in Chapter 3. A content analysis reveals the boundaries and structure of a content domain. The boundaries define the content domain as discrete from other domains of content. The structure defines the major sections of the content domain to be learned, the relationships between those sections, and the relative weight each section should receive in the total learning activity. Content objectives usually can be expressed in the cognitive domain as information to be acquired; they are most appropriate when it is not necessary to identify specific behaviors to be learned or when application of the content for problem solving is not desired.

Problem-Centered Objectives

Problem-centered objectives are those that identify a problem to be solved by the learner, and usually involve application of material learned in one context to the solution of a problem in another context. Some problems are very complex and require division into simpler problems or component behaviors (behavioral objectives). As learners become sophisticated, however, it is inappropriate to divide the problems into more specific behaviors to be learned. Examples of situations where problem-centered objectives would be appropriate arc communications, teamwork development, personal development, and resolution of specific problems in an organizational or community context.

Determining the Type of Objective to Use

Expressing objectives as behavioral, content, or problem-centered raises the question of the difference between goals and objectives. Generally stated, a goal represents a general desired outcome of the learning process for the learner, the organization, or the community. Objectives are more specific statements, several of which make up a goal. The dividing line between goals and objectives is arbitrary, depending on the complexity of the material to be learned and the sophistication of the learners. The learners' previous experience with the topic, their experience and skill as a learner, and their level of commitment to the learning process are all factors affecting the learner's level of sophistication.

The appropriateness of each type of objective can be determined by comparing the three learning domains to the level of sophistication of the learners. When dealing with cognitive learning outcomes and adult learners who lack sophistication, content objectives with very discrete elements of the content would appear to be well suited. More sophisticated learners could respond well to more complex content objectives or problem-centered objectives to learn cognitive material.

Learning affective material is usually demonstrated behaviorally, by identifying certain behaviors considered indicative of the desired attitude, value, or feeling to be learned. When educators work with learners who are not sophisticated, very discrete behavioral objectives are appropriate. With more sophisticated learners, more complex behavioral objectives or problem-centered objectives requiring the application or demonstration of attitudes are more appropriate.

When psychomotor skills are to be taught, it stands to reason that behavioral objectives of greater or lesser complexity, depending on the sophistication of the learners, would be appropriate. More sophisticated learners respond better to complex behavioral objectives or to problem-centered objectives that allow them to combine several behaviors to solve a problem or accomplish a task.

SEQUENCING GOALS AND OBJECTIVES

After identifying all the necessary goals and objectives, the next step is to sequence them. Preliminary sequencing of goals and objectives is described in this chapter. Final sequencing is accomplished after the learning activities have been developed, as discussed in Chapter 8. Several methods can be used to sequence goals and objectives: learning task analysis, chronological order, easiest to hardest, logical content sequence, first-to-last task, random order, and in accordance with learning domains:

1. *Learning task analysis*: The objectives are sequenced based on the order in which it is necessary to learn each skill (mastery of some skills requires prerequisite knowledge of other skills).

2. *Chronological order*: Arrange the objectives to reflect the order events occurred in history.

3. *Easiest to hardest*: Identify the level of difficulty involved in mastering all objectives and place them in order from the least difficult to the most difficult.

4. *Logical content sequence*: Identify a sequence of implicit or explicit topics that help the reader understand the content. For example, a teacher could group countries to be studied by geographic area or similarities in culture.

5. *First-to-last task*: Place the objectives in order from the first task to be accomplished to the last task in the series.

6. *Random order*: No particular order of the objectives is important, and they can be arranged in any order.

7. *Learning domain*: Arrange the objectives according to the domain. For example, all cognitive objectives could be grouped together, all affective objectives could be grouped together, and all psychomotor objectives could be grouped together.

Combinations of these approaches could be used in some situations. For example, learning domains could provide an overall structure for sequencing goals and objectives, while easiest to hardest could be used to sequence objectives within each learning domain. Sequencing objectives calls for preliminary judgments that will be further refined when learning activities designed to meet the objectives are developed.

INVOLVING LEARNERS IN DEVELOPING GOALS AND OBJECTIVES

The process described above may be forbidding even to experienced adult educators, let alone adult learners who were not hired for their expertise in instructional design. It seems apparent that learners should not be expected to master a complex instructional design process as well as the goals and objectives of the content. How, then, can learners be involved? Several suggestions for encouraging learner involvement are described below:

1. Involve learners in the needs assessment (discussed in more detail in Chapter 5); when possible, allow learners to take responsibility for their own needs assessment. Make them active partners in determining methods of needs assessment, attributes to be assessed, collecting and analyzing the data, and using the data to plan the learning activities.

2. Help learners become involved in task analysis. Some learners may have experience or expertise in one or more of the tasks to be learned—they can serve as resident experts.

3. Encourage learners to express learning goals in their own terms.

4. Encourage learners to analyze certification or licensure requirements to determine the goals and objectives needed to meet those requirements.

5. Involve learners in developing learning activities to meet the goals and objectives identified.

6. Involve learners in developing assessment procedures.

7. Have learners develop learning contracts, which will afford them the opportunity to become responsible for the instructional design process.

DEVELOPING GOALS AND OBJECTIVES: AN EXAMPLE

Application of instructional design allows you to engage in a structured planning process rather than relying on intuition, experience, or the whims of others, to develop an effective learning program. For example, assume you are responsible for developing a learning experience to help adult educators become effective group discussion leaders. Refer to Exhibit 3.1, Some Tasks and Skills of Group Discussion Leaders (in Chapter 3) in which procedural task analysis and learning task analysis were used to identify the tasks to be learned to be an effective discussion group leader. The example below builds on the process begun in Exhibit 3.1.

1. Conduct a task analysis of leading group discussions. The task analysis is based on a thorough description of leading discussion groups and should include the following:
   a. The roles of a group leader

b. Knowledge and skills required of a group leader
c. Typical patterns of behavior in a group
d. Desired outcomes of a group discussion
e. Physical arrangements for effective group discussions
f. Managing group discussions.

2. Conduct a learning task analysis in order to identify the goals which emerge from the tasks and the knowledge, attitudes, and skills required for each task. Goals that can be identified from Exhibit 3.1 are as follows:
   a. Knowledge of group roles
   b. Knowledge of group processes
   c. Knowledge of specific group facilitation techniques
   d. Knowledge of the content under discussion
   e. Belief in the value of participation
   f. Respect for the rights of others
   g. Ability to apply knowledge of group roles to lead discussion groups
   h. Ability to apply knowledge of group processes to lead discussion groups
   i. Ability to apply knowledge of group facilitation techniques to lead discussion groups

3. Identify the goals resulting from the contexts, licensure or certification requirements (if applicable), your strengths and needs as an adult educator, and the expressed and/or observed needs of the learners. These goals can then be combined with the goals identified in step 2 above and placed in a list from most important for the learners to least important. This will help determine which of the goals, if not all of them, can and should be met through the learning activities.

4. Divide the goals into the domains of the outcomes of learning. Goals a through e in step 2, above, are in the cognitive domain (information acquisition); goals e and f are in the affective domain; and goals g, h, and i are in the cognitive domain (problem solving). Any of these goals could be divided into more discrete goals depending on the level of sophistication of the learners. The two affective goals (e and f)

could be very difficult to teach if the learners resisted them. The last three goals (g, h, and i) are skills involving the application of knowledge and attitudes to achieve certain desired outcomes in the group process.

5. Develop learning objectives based on the goals identified. In Exhibit 7.1, Sample Goals and Objectives for Training Group Discussion Leaders, some of the tasks and skills identified in Exhibit 3.1 are translated into goals and objectives. Before writing the objectives, the level of sophistication of learners and the need for behavioral, content, or problem-centered objectives should be determined. In this example, a fairly high level of sophistication of the learners was assumed. For each objective, the terminal behavior, the conditions, and the criteria for performance are identified.

SUMMARY

The focus of this chapter has been on the process of developing learning goals and objectives. Usually, each goal can be divided into several objectives and can be developed based on desired learning outcomes (from a task or content analysis), licensure or certification requirements, the learning contexts, the instructor's strengths and needs, and the learners' observed or expressed needs.

Of the three types of objectives, behavioral objectives are most useful when specific skills or attitudes are to be learned. Content objectives are most useful when the desired outcome is information acquisition, and problem-centered objectives are most useful for learning to apply knowledge to solve problems.

Identifying appropriate goals and objectives is the most important part of the entire instructional design process. Appropriate goals and objectives will aid in developing effective learning activities; inappropriate ones will result in learning activities which do not meet the needs of the learners or the sponsoring institution or agency and do not reflect the content. Developing learning activities is the subject of the next chapter.

EXHIBIT 7.1
Sample Goals and Objectives for
Training Group Discussion Leaders

Domain	Selected Goals	Sample Objectives	Type of Objective
Cognitive (Information)	Knowledge of group roles	In a group discussion, LWBAT* identify all of the major roles played by group members.	Content
Affective	Belief in the value of participation	In an essay test, LWBAT identify and discuss five uses of group discussion as a learning method.	Content
		In a group discussion, LWBAT identify and discuss five possible benefits of group discussion for individual learners.	Content
		In a group discussion, LWBAT identify and discuss three possible negative outcomes for individuals resulting from participation in discussion groups.	Content

Domain	Selected Goals	Sample Objectives	Type of Objective
Cognitive (Problem Solving)	Ability to apply group facilitation techniques to lead group discussions	In a role play situation, LWBAT successfully demonstrate appropriate attentive body language.	Problem Solving
		In a role play situation, LWBAT accurately restate feelings expressed by others.	Problem Solving
		In a classroom setting, LWBAT lead a discussion group using Nominal Group Technique.	Problem Solving
		In a role play situation, LWBAT effectively demonstrate techniques for encouraging participation in the discussion by reluctant participants.	Problem Solving

*LWBAT = Learner will be able to

CHAPTER 8

Developing Learning Activities

A learning activity is a set of structured experiences designed to help learners achieve one or more learning objectives. Learning activities are usually considered to be the heart and soul of helping adults learn. Many books in adult education focus on facilitating learning activities, emphasizing the importance of the nature of the contact between the adult educator and the learner (i.e., Bergevin, Morris, & Smith, 1963; Galbraith, 1991, 1998; Seaman, 1977; Seaman & Fellenz, 1989). The planning of learning activities is often portrayed as tangential, if it is discussed at all.

In traditional instructional design models, the development of learning activities is driven by content rather than the needs of the learners. Given the emphasis in adult education on facilitating learning, this content emphasis may account, at least in part, for lack of widespread adoption of instructional design by adult educators. The prevailing wisdom appears to be that being a good facilitator of learning is the most important aspect of being an effective adult educator.

In fact, developing effective learning activities is basic to having successful face-to-face contact with adult learners. In this chapter, three steps in developing learning activities are considered: selecting learning activities, constructing learning activities, and sequencing learning activities.

SELECTING LEARNING ACTIVITIES

Several factors to consider when determining which learning methods to use are listed in Exhibit 8.1, Factors to Consider

---

EXHIBIT 8.1
Factors to Consider When Selecting Learning Activities

---

1. Are the learning activities appropriate for the objectives?

2. Do the learning activities reflect the desired degree of learner involvement?

3. What is your level of experience and comfort in facilitating these learning activities?

4. How much preparation time is needed for each learning activity?

5. Do these types of activities meet the expectations of the learners?

6. How much preparation is needed by the adult learners for these learning activities?

7. How complex are the activities to conduct? Is that level of complexity appropriate for the learners?

8. How much time will the activities take to execute?

9. Will you need special equipment or facilities for the activities?

10. Do these types of activities meet the expectations of the sponsoring organization, decision makers, and/or community values?

When Selecting Learning Activities. It will be noted that the questions in Exhibit 8.1 reflect input from all areas of assessment: assessment of yourself as an adult educator, assessment of the content to be learned, assessment of the context in which learning takes place, as well as assessment of the needs of the adult learners.

Before selecting different learning activities, however, it is useful to be aware of the options you have. Exhibit 8.2, Methods

---

EXHIBIT 8.2
Methods and Techniques for Adult Learners

Action Groups	Individualized Instruction
Apprenticeship	Institute
Audience Reaction Team	Internship
Brainstorming	Interview
Buzz Session	Learning Contracts
Case Study	Lecture
Colloquy	Listening Teams
Committee	Mentoring
Computer Aided Instruction	Microteaching
Conference	Newsletters
Convention	Nominal Group Technique
Correspondence Study	Panel
Critical Incident	Participation Training
Debate	Practice
Demonstration	Programmed Instruction
Exhibit	Psychodrama
Field Trip	Role Play
Forum	Simulation
Games	Skit
Group Discussion	Symposium
In-Basket Exercise	Television
Independent Study	Workshop

---

and Techniques for Adult Learners, lists a variety of methods and techniques to consider when constructing learning activities. These methods and techniques are more fully described in the following books: *Adult Learning Methods* edited by Galbraith (1998), *Effective Strategies for Teaching Adults* by Seaman and Fellenz (1989), *Adult Education Teaching Techniques* by Seaman (1977), and *A Handbook of Tested Patterns for Effective Participation* by Bergevin, Morris, and Smith (1963).

After addressing the issues raised in Exhibit 8.1, there are two primary factors to consider in the selection of different types of learning methods: domains of learning and the level of learner involvement. You will recall that objectives can be placed into one of three different learning domains: cognitive, affective, and psychomotor. Further, the cognitive domain can be divided into two levels: information acquisition and problem solving. Some learning activities are better suited to meeting objectives in one of the learning domains than others. For example, lecture is better suited to information acquisition than it is to the development of psychomotor skills.

The second consideration is the level of learner involvement. It has become an axiom in adult education that learners should be involved in the learning process; that is, learners should be active not passive. Therefore, it is important to select learning activities which promote active learning. In general, learning activities can be divided into three levels of learner involvement. With low levels of learner involvement, such as lecture, learners are completely passive; they are merely receptacles who listen to and receive information presented by an instructor. Moderate levels of learner involvement, such as panel presentations and interviews, offer learners opportunities for interaction through asking questions or making comments. Lastly, in high levels of learner involvement, such as in simulation games and role plays, learners are afforded the opportunity to learn by doing; that is, they are actively engaged in learning.

Learners react differently to engaging in active learning. Some learners are eager to jump in and interact while others are reticent for a variety of reasons. Some may be threatened by high levels of involvement when they lack self-confidence or self-esteem and when they feel forced to perform in front of peers or strangers. Under these circumstances, it may be best to avoid high levels of involvement in the early stages of instruction. One strategy to overcome this problem is to begin with activities characterized by low levels of learner involvement and introduce higher levels of learner involvement when the learners are "warmed up." Another strategy is to introduce the learners to active learning with activities that are noncompetitive. Educators can also encourage learners to be supportive of one another so that a nonthreatening atmosphere is created.

In Figure 8.1, these two factors, learning domains and learner involvement, are juxtaposed to help identify appropriate learning methods and techniques. The four principal domains are listed on the left, creating rows in which learning methods and techniques appropriate for different domains are displayed. The three levels of learner involvement are listed across the top, creating columns of learning methods and techniques that promote that level of learner involvement. Each cell in the diagram, then, has learning methods and techniques which can be used to promote a specific level of learner involvement to reach objectives in each of the domains. Selecting the appropriate methods and techniques to use as a basis for your learning activities, then, becomes a matter of using judgment about which methods and techniques are appropriate for the domain and level of learner involvement desired.

CONSTRUCTING LEARNING ACTIVITIES

In this section, the essential components of successful learning activities are identified and developing learning activities is discussed. Though developing a lecture is quite a different type of activity from developing a case study or simulation game, there are some generic steps which can be used to structure most learning activities.

According to Gagne, Briggs, and Wager (1988), there are nine events of instruction that should occur in each learning activity: (1) gaining attention, (2) informing the learner of the objective, (3) stimulating recall of prerequisite learning, (4) presenting the stimulus material, (5) providing learning guidance, (6) eliciting the performance, (7) providing feedback about the performance, (8) assessing the performance, and (9) enhancing retention and transfer.

Adult educators will discover that actual components of each learning activity will vary depending upon type of activity and learning domain. However, a modified version of Gagne, Briggs, and Wager's (1988) events of instruction, depicted in

Levels of Learner Involvement

Domains of Learning	Low	Medium	High
Cognitive (Problem solving)	Demonstration Debate Television	Panel Interview	Role Play/Simulation Case Study In-Basket Exercise Computer Aided Instruction
Cognitive (Information Acquisition)	Lecture Exhibit Television	Panel Interview Debate	Field Trip Computer Aided Instruction
Affective	Lecture Exhibit Demonstration Television	Panel Interview Debate Computer Aided Instruction	Case Study Simulation Role Play Group Discussion
Psychomotor	Demonstration Television	Demonstration with Practice	

Figure 8.1 Sample Methods and Techniques to Enhance Learner Involvement

Exhibit 8.3, Components of Learning Activities, can be used to construct many learning activities for adult education.

Components of Learning Activities

The components of learning activities listed in Exhibit 8.3 are described in more detail below.

Introduction

The introduction serves to gain the learners' attention and focus them on the task at hand. Goals and objectives for the learning activity usually are made explicit here, if that has not already been done. Learners can also be helped to recall prior learning applicable to the current learning activity in the introduction.

Introductions are usually short, not more than a few minutes. If more time is called for (for example, extensive recall of prior learning), then the learning activity may be too complex for one session and need to be divided into two or more discrete learning activities.

Directions

When minimal directions for a learning activity are required, it may be necessary only to set the parameters for it. For example, if the activity is a lecture, directions may be simply informing the learners how long the lecture will last and what topics will be addressed. More complex activities require more complex directions.

Directions should be clear and concise. When several steps are involved, using both written and verbal presentation of the directions is usually best. This may be done with handouts, a chalkboard, a flip chart, an overhead projector, a PowerPoint presentation, or any other easily visible way. Also, directions should be presented in the order in which they are to be completed. Throughout the learning activity, the instructor should

EXHIBIT 8.3
Components of Learning Activities

Component	Purpose
Introduction	Gain the learners' attention; inform them of the purpose (goals and objectives) of the activity; stimulate recall of prior learning needed for the activity.
Directions	Inform the learner of the directions, rules, and/or guidelines for completing the activity.
Activity	Present to the learners or have the learners engage in the learning activity.
Practice and Feedback	Practice the skill, recite the knowledge, or display the desired behavior identified in the objectives.
Retention and Transfer	Retain the material learned and transfer it to other settings.

assess the learners' attentiveness, and directions should be re-stated as necessary.

Learning Activity

Once the introduction and directions have been made explicit, the learning activity can commence. During learning activities, the instructor should observe the learners constantly to determine if they understand what is happening and if the timing, pace, level of complexity, and content are appropriate. When learners are passive, as at lectures and exhibits, instructors must be aware of learner receptivity to the presentation. Waning interest usually indicates that a change of pace, content, or level of learner involvement is needed.

In activities with moderate levels of learner involvement, like panels, interviews, and field trips, learners are active some times and passive other times. Monitoring is necessary to ensure that learners are attentive during periods of passivity so that they may participate fully during both the active and passive periods.

High involvement learning activities, such as discussions, demonstrations and practice, case studies, simulations, and role plays require that learners be involved in all phases of the learning activity. The instructor must monitor learners to determine that they understand the goals, objectives, and directions of the activity and keep focused on the intended outcomes. It is important that learners do not concentrate solely on the activity itself and lose sight of why they are doing it. Another note of caution—learning can be strenuous and prolonged levels of high involvement can produce fatigue. Monitor learners for potential fatigue and if necessary, offer frequent breaks or make adjustments in the schedule of learning activities.

Practice and Feedback

Practice and feedback may or may not be an integral part of the learning activity. For example, a lecture may not have a practice component. If a lecture is followed by an activity during which learners are expected to apply concepts learned from the lecture, then practice and feedback become part of the learning activity. In high involvement learning activities, practice and feedback often are integral. For example, a role play may involve learners in practicing certain behaviors and receiving feedback from other learners.

Retention and Transfer

"Retention" means assimilating the new learning into the long-term memory so that it can be recalled in the future. "Transfer" means being able to apply information learned in one context, such as a classroom, to another context, such as on the job. Often, encouraging retention and transfer of learning is the most difficult part of a learning activity because a long-term relationship must be maintained with the learner to assist in retention and transfer. Transferring learning is also difficult when the context to which the learning is being transferred is hostile and does not support the transfer process. This situation is typified by remarks like, "that may be the way you learned it in school, but this is the real world."

To assist in retention and transfer, adult educators can encourage the learners to relate the new material to their previous experiences, their jobs, or other appropriate aspects of their lives. The educator can help the learners anticipate obstacles to transferring new material; anticipated obstacles may be dealt with more easily than unanticipated ones. Retention and transference are assisted also when learners are actively involved in the learning process and have practiced the skills. Active learners tend to learn skills more thoroughly and, therefore, confidence to employ the skills is increased.

Constructing Learning Activities

The steps in constructing learning activities are the following:

1. State the goals and learning objectives for the learning activity.

2. Identify the domains of learning involved in meeting the objectives.

3. Determine the level of involvement desired of the learners in the learning activity.

4. Select one or more types of learning activities.

5. Determine the amount of time needed and available for the activity.

6. Develop an outline of the activity.

7. Write the content of the activity.

8. Develop the directions needed for the learners.

9. Determine the supporting equipment and facilities needed for the activity.

10. Develop supporting materials for the activity such as handouts and overhead transparencies.

A more detailed description of developing experiential learning activities is contained in *Enhancing Organizational Effectiveness in Adult and Community Education* by Dean, Murk, and Del Prete (2000). The model employed in this book contains seven steps. The roles of the instructor and learner are addressed in each step.

Often, the person developing the activity will not be responsible for the instruction. When this is the case—and even when it is not—a detailed plan is helpful to those who deliver the learning activity. The plan usually contains the 10 items listed above arranged so that they can be easily followed. A one-page organizer is a useful tool to provide an overview of the learning activity. The organizer should contain the title of the learning activity, the instructor(s), the place the learning activity has in the overall sequence, the amount of time needed for the activity, the goal met through the activity, the objectives met through the activity, a brief description of the learning activity, the evaluation procedures, equipment or facilities needed, and other comments such as safety concerns or transportation requirements. An example of such a one-page description is shown in Figure 8.2, Learning Activity Organizer. Other information such as lecture notes, handouts for the learners, overhead transparencies, assessment devices, and worksheets can be included as addenda.

SEQUENCING LEARNING ACTIVITIES

Sequencing learning activities is the final step in the process of developing them. In this stage it is important to think about

LEARNING ACTIVITY ORGANIZER

Title:_____

Activity_____ of_____   Time Needed:_____

Instructor(s):_____
_____

Goals:_____
_____

Objectives:_____
_____
_____

Description of Learning Activity:_____
_____
_____
_____
_____

Evaluation Procedures:_____
_____
_____
_____

Equipment, Material, and Facilities Needed:_____
_____
_____
_____

Notes:_____
_____
_____
_____

Figure 8.2 Learning Activity Organizer

the whole process of instruction: the learning activities viewed in relationship to the goals and objectives, the characteristics and needs of the learners, the desired levels of learner involvement, your ability to manage the learning process, the availability of facilities and equipment, and the time required for each activity.

Each of the following approaches to sequencing learning activities can be used to enhance learner involvement: (1) begin with activities which require low levels of involvement and build to higher levels of involvement, (2) begin with a high level of involvement and maintain it, (3) alternate between high and low levels of involvement, (4) begin with a high level of involvement and end with a low level of involvement, and (5) maintain low levels of involvement throughout the learning process. Options 1, 2, and 3 would appear to offer the most promise for developing learner involvement and commitment to the learning process. Options 4 and 5 would have use only under special circumstances.

Final sequencing of learning activities is obviously a balancing act between the various considerations discussed above. In the end, there may be more than one "best way" to sequence learning activities. Following are some guidelines that can be useful:

1. Allow sufficient time for learning activities with high levels of learner involvement; managing the logistics of such activities often takes more time than anticipated.

2. Allow sufficient breaks, especially when there are intense activities or long periods of learning.

3. Monitor learner attentiveness and participation to ensure that you are with your learners and that they are with you.

4. Make sure in advance that facilities and equipment are available when and where they are needed and that they work properly.

DEVELOPING A LEARNING ACTIVITY:
AN EXAMPLE

Following is an example of how to develop a learning activity. The example is based on the goals and objectives developed in Chapter 7, Exhibit 7.1, for teaching discussion group leaders. Using the 10-step process outlined on pages 98–99, a learning activity for one of the objectives identified in Exhibit 7.1 is developed as follows:

1. Goal: Ability to apply group facilitation techniques to lead group discussions.

   Objective: In a role play situation, learners will be able to effectively demonstrate techniques for encouraging participation in the discussion by learners, some of whom may be reluctant participants.

2. Domain: Cognitive, problem solving.

3. Level of involvement: high (a skill is being learned that needs to be practiced).

4. Type of learning activity: role play (this type of activity, which is relatively risk-free, allows learners to practice skills without embarrassment or possible damage to themselves or others).

5. Time: approximately 1 1/2 hours.

6. Outline of Activity:

   I. Introduction (10 minutes).
      A. State goals and objectives for the activity.
      B. Recall prior learning needed for the activity.
   II. Directions (overview of the structure of the activity, 5 minutes).
   III. Activity (40 minutes).
      A. Lecture (introduction of the concepts, 10 minutes).
      B. Demonstration of the concepts (10 minutes).
      C. Small group role play activity (practice and feedback, 25 minutes).

IV. Conclusion (discussion of practice and use of skill in other settings, 30 minutes).

7. Content: A script or extensive notes based on the brief outline in item 6 above should be developed.

8. Directions: The directions for the learning activity should be chronological, clear, and concise.

9. Supporting equipment and facilities: overhead projector and screen; a large room with movable furniture (tables and chairs) and/or small break-out rooms with movable furniture.

10. Supporting materials: overhead transparencies for lecture on principles of restatement, script for demonstration of restatement, and roles printed as handouts for learners to practice restatement technique.

SUMMARY

Developing learning activities is both a science and an art—the first stems from the techniques described in this chapter and the entire instructional design process, while the latter stems from one's experience and personal characteristics. The systematic instructional design approach can be used as a framework upon which one's experience and characteristics are built, evaluated, and enhanced.

Important items to consider in developing learning activities include selecting activities appropriate to learners, content, contexts, and strengths and weaknesses of the adult educator; constructing each activity to meet specific objectives; and selecting and sequencing activities to achieve the desired levels of learner involvement.

Learning activities provide the vehicle to reach the outcomes stated in goals and objectives. Evaluation determines if the outcomes have been reached. Developing learner evaluation is discussed in the next chapter.

CHAPTER 9

Evaluating Learners

The topic of this chapter, evaluating learners, causes headaches and heartaches for many adult educators and learners. Adult educators are often torn between the notion that evaluation is antithetical to their philosophy or style of teaching and the fact that they are forced to play the heavy by evaluating learners when they teach. The purpose of this chapter is to explore how evaluation can be designed with more positive results for learners and less pain all the way around. We will focus on four major issues: the purposes of evaluation, what should be evaluated, the timing of evaluation, and methods of evaluation.

WHY EVALUATE LEARNERS

Guba and Lincoln (1982) defined evaluation as determining the value or worth of something. The underlying purpose of learner evaluation is to ascertain the degree to which learners have acquired the goals and objectives. Discovering the learner's competence also serves the purpose:

1. to increase the learner's self-awareness and potential for personal and professional growth;

2. to increase the learner's self-confidence and commitment to learning;

3. to improve communication between learners and adult educators so that they may work more effectively together;

4. to help determine the future direction and pace of learning; and

5. to award credentials such as grades, credits, certificates, licenses, and diplomas.

In a particular learning situation, one or more of these reasons may affect directly the nature of the evaluation conducted. Often the reasons for conducting evaluation are taken for granted: the adult educator is told which evaluation method will be used, history and tradition dictate a certain evaluative process, certification or licensure requirements mandate certain types of evaluation, or adult educators use evaluation methods they have experienced in the past.

WHAT TO EVALUATE

While the type of learning to be evaluated may appear self-evident, during a systematic examination of the learning situation, the adult educator may discover much more worth evaluating than is first apparent. But what system for identifying what to evaluate is most effective? Kirkpatrick (1987) identified a four-area system for evaluation of training programs: (1) reaction of the learners to the program; (2) knowledge, skills, and attitudes learned; (3) changes in job behavior resulting from the training; and (4) tangible results of the training program for the organization. Gagne, Briggs, and Wager (1988) suggest that evaluation should be determined by the five outcomes of instruction they identified: intellectual skills, cognitive strategies, verbal information, motor skills, and attitudes. Combining these two evaluation schemes results in identifying the following areas for evaluation:

1. learners' reactions to the learning experience;

2. information;

3. problem-solving skills;

4. psychomotor skills;

5. affective factors such as attitudes, values, and feelings;

6. personal growth and development; and

7. changes in the organization or community.

Items 1 and 7 above are examples of indirect indicators of learning. Item 1, the learners' reactions, is discussed more fully in Chapter 10. Item 7 relies on identifying changes in the organization or community that result from the accumulated changes in learners' behavior. For example, a new production technology successfully learned by employees in a training program may result in increased productivity, or a community safe sex program may result in fewer cases of AIDS in that community. Because the connection between the data indicating changes in the organization or community and the learning program is often tenuous, this type of evaluation is often difficult and expensive to conduct, and is usually beyond the means of adult educators working with limited time, expertise, and budgets.

Items 2 through 6 are the areas usually identified for evaluation. Each brings to mind different methods of evaluation conducted at different times. Item 2, evaluating information, is often a matter of testing the learner's ability to recall facts acquired during the learning process. Evaluating problem-solving skills, item 3, calls for learners to apply newly acquired information and strategies to new situations. Item 4, psychomotor skills, is frequently evaluated through observation or skill tests, in which learners are expected to demonstrate certain behaviors with some specified degree of accuracy. Affective learning, item 5, is often more difficult to evaluate, but it can be useful to have learners demonstrate behaviors or make decisions indicative of the desired attitudes or values being learned. Item 6, personal growth and development, is perhaps the most difficult area to evaluate. Often anecdotal evidence or self-reports from learners are the only methods available to substantiate personal growth. Adult educators who have an extended relationship with learners can sometimes observe personal growth and development, but unless there are systematic means developed for observing personal growth, evidence for it is usually incomplete and subjective.

Long (1990) suggested a holistic evaluation process which

consists of three categories for evaluation: (1) primary learning, which addresses the specific goals and objectives of the learning program, (2) associated learning, which is a content or skill and a corollary of the learner's pursuit of the primary learning objectives, and (3) attendant learning, which is affective and focuses on self-revelation as a result of participating in the learning experience. Integrating Long's evaluation model with the list of areas for evaluation cited above creates a framework in which adult educators and learners can share in a holistic learning process directly related to the goals, objectives, and domains of learning. The following approach would result from such an integration of the models:

1. Primary learning: mastering the goals and objectives of the learning activity expressed as information, problem-solving skills, psychomotor skills, and attitudes, values, and beliefs.

2. Associated learning: acquiring information, problem-solving skills, psychomotor skills, and attitudes, values, and beliefs in addition to the stated goals and objectives for the learning activity.

3. Attendant learning: personal growth of the learner, self-awareness, and awareness of others, which results from participation in the learning process.

WHEN TO EVALUATE

The timing of evaluation may appear to be self-evident—it is done when the learning is over. In fact, evaluation can take place during four broad time periods: before the learning takes place, during learning, immediately following learning, and at some time after the learning has been completed. The nature of the evaluative process changes with each time period.

Evaluation conducted before learning takes place is usually referred to as learner needs assessment and is discussed in detail in Chapter 5. Conducting evaluation prior to learning can be used to develop course content and learning activities and also to develop individual learning contracts. Needs assessment is evaluation to the extent that learner knowledge and competence related to the learning goals and objectives are identified.

Evaluation conducted during the learning process usually serves two purposes. First, it helps the adult educator keep in touch with the learners so that the material is not covered too fast or too slow. Second, changes in the learning material and activities can be made as indicated by the reactions of the learners to what has transpired thus far.

Evaluation conducted at the end of a course, workshop, or program is the most typical time frame. It is usually accomplished with a test, written or otherwise, through which learners are expected to demonstrate knowledge, attitudes, and skills acquired through the learning process.

Delayed evaluation can occur when it is important to check the learners' retention of material over time and/or their ability to apply it in different settings. This is often difficult to accomplish because the learners may no longer be accessible. When it is possible, however, delayed evaluation may provide the most telling information about what has been learned, what is most useful to the learners, and changes needed in the learning activities for the future.

HOW TO EVALUATE

Evaluation of adult learners can be informal or formal. Informal evaluation (1) helps learners learn about themselves (develop self-awareness), (2) helps learners develop self-confidence and commitment to learning, (3) ensures effective communication between learners and adult educators, and (4) helps modify learning activities for and with learners as needed. This type of evaluation is accomplished through observation of learners or in one-on-one and group discussions. Formal evaluation can accomplish all the goals identified under informal evaluation and, in addition, allows institutions and organizations to award credentials such as grades, credits, certificates, licenses, and diplomas to learners, and often is accomplished through testing. Some frequently used methods of evaluation are discussed below.

Objective Written Tests

An objective test is an instrument which is administered and scored the same way regardless of who takes, administers, or scores it. This means that there are standard rules for administration and scoring the test. Typical items on objective tests are multiple choice, matching, true-false, and fill-in-the-blank. Examples of these types of items appear in Chapter 5. The advantages of objective tests is that they can be administered by a proctor, are easy to score, and can be effective fr evaluating information acquired by the learners and some problem-solving types of learning. They are, however, often time consuming to develop, and some learners have difficulty with the format. Also, psychomotor skills, affective factors, personal growth, and some types of problem solving are not readily measured by objective tests.

Sometimes, objective tests are mandated by institutions to ensure mastery of a topic so that a credential can be issued to the learner. The underlying logic here is that objective tests are the only fair way to determine that all learners have mastered the appropriate material. Further, it is argued, use of objective tests removes bias from the grading process. A major flaw in this line of reasoning is the assumption that all learners are equally able to demonstrate learning through objective tests. Another flaw is the assumption that objective tests are truly "objective" in what they measure; even if the content domain boundary and structure method is used, material measured on objective tests has been subjectively determined by the instructor.

Objective tests can be given before the learning activity as a needs assessment, during learning to ensure that learners are on track, and after learning to determine the amount of material learned. While usually considered a formal means of evaluation, objective tests can be used for informal evaluation when the scores are not for determining competence or for awarding credentials. In these situations it is usually best to have learners grade their own tests so that they learn from the results. A private discussion between learners and the adult educator may be needed to ensure growth from the testing experience.

Developing objective written tests can be difficult and time consuming. According to McKeachie (1994) there are several guidelines for developing objective tests. Of the various items available, McKeachie recommends multiple-choice as the most useful. They are able to measure cognitive knowledge as well as discrimination and some problem solving. He suggests that sources of multiple-choice items include teachers' manuals and the students themselves. He provided several rules for writing multiple-choice items: (1) each problem should be a single issue, (2) use brief statements, not complex sentences, (3) use positive statements not negative statements, (4) problem statements should make sense without reading the alternatives, and (5) use concrete rather than abstract terms. He also developed rules for writing the alternatives: (1) right answers should be unquestionably right (checked by several people), (2) wrong answers should represent mistakes commonly made by your students not the public at large, (3) answers should be brief, (4) vary the position of the right answer, (5) place numerical answers in order, (6) do not use words unfamiliar to your students, (7) use "all of the above" and "none of the above" rarely, and (8) do not provide irrelevant clues to the right answer (such as using "never" or "always" in wrong answers, more elaborate statements for the right answer, or grammatical inconsistencies which point out the right or wrong answers).

Determining the number and proportion of items on an objective test is a matter of judgment. McKeachie (1994) suggests that about one minute per multiple-choice item should be allowed for students to complete the test. The proportion of items can be determined through content analysis (as described in Chapter 3). Questions to keep in mind while developing an objective test are "Does it measure the objectives?" and "Are the students adequately prepared for this type of test?"

Subjective Written Tests

Evaluation by subjective tests requires a judgment by the scorer to determine a grade. Essay exams are the primary example of subjective paper and pencil tests. In-class essay exams usually emphasize a strong element of recall as well as application of the material (problem solving). Take-home essay exams emphasize application of material and not recall. Also, affective factors, such as attitudes, values, and beliefs can be observed through essay tests.

Essay tests are usually administered after a certain amount of learning has occurred because the synthesis and application of the material required by the test relies upon complete understanding of the material. Therefore, a primary purpose of essay tests is to certify mastery of some material in order to award a credential. Another use of essay exams is to promote learner self-understanding and awareness. This is effective because the act of writing requires both synthesis of information and generation of ideas in forms appropriate to written language; therefore, the learner engages with the material in a new way and thereby produces "new" learning.

Developing an essay test is usually much easier than developing an objective test. Essays can be composed of "short-answer" or "long-answer" questions. Short-answer essay questions usually measure informational objectives by requiring the learner to define or describe something. Long-answer essay questions can be composed to elicit higher order cognitive processes such as application of information to solve problems. Students can be asked to compare, contrast, provide examples, explain, and describe ideas and events in detail. Essay questions, whether short- or long-answer, should be written clearly and briefly.

Role Plays and Simulations

Role plays, simulations, and games are learning methods that can also be used as evaluation tools. Role plays are situations in which learners, usually in a group, assume certain characteristics and act as if the they were their own. A simulation is a structured set of activities through which learners become immersed in a process to gain an understanding of certain dynamics. A game is a simulation with winners and losers. All three techniques can be used to promote learner self-awareness, increase learner self-confidence and commitment to learning, increase teacher-learner communications, predict future learning, and award credentials. They are also useful for predicting future learning and modifying future learning activities. As learners participate in the activities, the adult educator can observe behavior and determine what objectives should be addressed next in the course and how best to address those objectives. Therefore, role plays, simulations, and games can be applied both in summary evaluation after the learning has occurred and in formative assessment in the middle of the learning process.

Bergevin, Morris, and Smith (1963) noted that there are several steps in developing and conducting role plays. Before the role play the facilitator should: (1) carefully assess the group's relevant characteristics such as age, gender, background, and attitudes; (2) define the problem and visualize to the learners the situation to be played; (3) select the roles to be played; (4) decide on the order in which the "scenes" will be played and how many times they will be played; (5) cast the characters; (6) brief the players on their roles; and (7) arrange the facilities and equipment needed to conduct the role play. During the role-play activity, the facilitator should: (1) introduce the role-play scenario to the learners; (2) begin the role play; (3) stop the action when it is appropriate; (4) "release" the actors from their roles by having them comment on how they felt; (5) initiate a replay of the role play if necessary; and (6) conduct an analysis of the role play with all of the learners.

Gilley (1998) defined a simulation as "a technique which enables adult learners to obtain skills, competencies, knowledge, or behaviors, by becoming involved in situations that are similar to those in real life" (p. 272). Through simulations the learners are involved in complex problems or issues about which they learn both cognitively and affectively. Simulations engage the learners in acting out roles in carefully prescribed settings which "simulate" some real situation. Often the learners are placed at odds with one another so that they must learn to cope with conflicting roles while trying to reach certain objectives within the simulation process. Gilley has outlined some guidelines for facilitators of simulations which should occur before the simulation begins: (1) provide clear instructions to the learners (including the roles, dialog, and problem to be addressed); (2) identify the context and objectives of the simulation; (3) provide the resources needed for the simulation; and (4) structure the sequence of activities. During the simulation, Gilley stated that the facilitator should provide essential feedback at critical points to either individuals or groups, encourage the learners, and clarify directions when needed.

Case Studies

Case studies are situations that require development of a solution, and are good tools for evaluating problem-solving skills. Learners need to identify the relevant characteristics in the case study, understand the dynamics, and develop one or more strategies for coping with the situation described.

Case studies can be used during or at the end of a learning activity. For evaluation purposes, case studies can be used during learning to assess understanding of concepts in order to modify future or present learning activities. At the end, they help certify competence for awarding credentials based on learner performance. In addition, case studies can help learners learn more about themselves; they are especially helpful for learner self-awareness when used in small group settings.

Marsick (1998) noted that there are three aspects to case studies—the report, analysis, and discussion. The report is the case study itself. Marsick identifies several steps in developing case studies: (1) identify a problem which is real, typical, complex, and researchable; (2) dramatize the problem so that the learners understand and can relate to the characters as well as the problem; (3) keep the learners' level of sophistication and experience in mind when developing the case study; (4) tailor the case study to the time, purpose, and place in the course; and (5) develop the administrative and support materials needed to use the case study.

Observation

Observation is the process of paying close attention to learners' verbal and nonverbal behavior during a learning activity. Adult educators should use observation as an informal evaluation technique for keeping in touch with the learners at all times during the learning process; when learners are fatigued, bewildered, frustrated, impatient, or inattentive, the educator can make modifications to the learning activities. Adult educators also conduct observations when they need to know if they and the learners are working together to accomplish the stated goals and objectives.

Formal observations can be conducted to determine the competency of learners. To do this adult educators construct elaborate lists of skills or desired behaviors and levels of competency for each skill or behavior to guide the observation. Formal observations may be conducted in a clinic or practicum where learners demonstrate certain skills, or in a natural setting. For example, supervisors may observe employees applying skills on the job that they have recently learned in a training program.

Demonstration

Demonstration is a process in which learners observe, practice, and then perform a skill. Demonstration is useful for evaluating psychomotor skills and some problem-solving applications, and often is used to ensure learner competence in certain skills for the purpose of awarding credentials. When sufficient time and coaching have been allowed for practice before the evaluative demonstration, demonstration can also help the learner build confidence.

According to Laird (1985) a demonstrator has the following responsibilities: (1) analyze the process to be demonstrated and break it into small steps; (2) have all of the materials for the demonstration in place; (3) check all equipment before the demonstration; (4) arrange the demonstration so all the learners can see it; (5) explain the goals at the beginning in a two-way discussion with the learner; (6) present the demonstration one step at a time and explain each step as it occurs; (7) allow the learners to practice the skill, procedure, or behavior at the earliest possible time; and (8) reinforce everything the learners do correctly.

Journals

Journals are written records made during or after the learning experience. They are effective as evaluative tools to track learner ability to synthesize information and to identify personal growth and affective factors. Usually they are kept throughout the learning process and evaluated periodically by the adult educator. The primary purpose of a journal is to help learners increase their self-awareness and commitment to learning. They can also be used to increase effective communication between the learners and the adult educator.

While journals may assume a great variety of shapes and sizes, there are some guidelines for writing them. First, since journals usually contain self-revealing information, the contents of a person's journal should be kept confidential. Individuals should not feel even the slightest pressure to show their journals to other students or anyone else. Second, students should be given a topic or theme to guide their comments in the journal. Comments will usually be self-reflective, so the theme of the journal should encourage students to relate the material being learned to their personal and/or professional development. Third, expectations should be given as to length, format, and due dates. Students should be encouraged to consult the instructor while writing their journals. Consultations can serve (1) to help students talk-through and identify their thoughts and feelings to be recorded in the journal; (2) to clarify instructions or expectations for the journal; and (3) to help identify and refer students for additional assistance if needed.

Learner-Developed Assessments

At times it is appropriate for learners to develop their own evaluation procedures. For example, one learner may want to write a paper, another to present an oral report, and a third to do an activity outside of class. The type of assessment procedures developed will depend on the type of learning project initiated by the student, and are often the result of individual learning contracts developed between the learner and the adult educator. Since the learning and assessment procedures which can be used are open, they can serve any of the stated purposes for evaluation.

GUIDELINES FOR LEARNER EVALUATION

As important as the purpose, type, method, and timing of evaluation, is the spirit in which it is done. Evaluation given in a mean or demeaning way can do more damage than is imagined. Evaluation done in a spirit of helpfulness and understanding can enhance learning and be beneficial to all involved. Following are some guidelines to help ensure that evaluation is positive and not destructive.

1. Praise can be given in public or private, but criticism should always be given in private. Further, criticism should be constructive, not destructive; comments should help the learner identify how to improve. Evaluation should be of learning gains; the learners should not be made to feel unworthy because they have not mastered certain learning objectives.

2. Allow learners the opportunity to evaluate your teaching. Their evaluation should not be pro forma and the learners

should be made aware of how their evaluations of you will be used.

3. Involve the learners in the process of developing and implementing the evaluation as much as is possible. When feasible, let them determine how they will be evaluated and the criteria used for success.

4. When evaluation is predetermined and the learners have little or no part in the process, then they should be aware of methods of evaluation, the timing of evaluation, and the criteria used for determining success from the beginning of the learning process.

5. The learners must understand how the evaluation can help them and how they can apply the information learned from the evaluation in the future.

SUMMARY

Evaluation can be immensely beneficial or very devastating to adult learners, depending on how it is conducted. Evaluation is intended to discover if the learners have mastered certain learning goals and objectives, but it can also negate learning. Determining learner competence also serves: (1) to increase learners' potential for personal and professional growth, (2) to increase learners' self-confidence and commitment to learning, (3) to improve communications between learners and adult educators, (4) to help decide the future direction and pace of learning, and (5) to award grades, credits, certificates, licenses, and diplomas. Areas that can be evaluated before, during, or after the learning activity include learners' reactions to participating in the learning experience, information, problem-solving skills, psychomotor skills, attitudes acquired by the learners, learners' personal growth, and changes in the community or organization which result from the learning experience. For a more thorough discussion of evaluation, see Moran, *Assessing Adult Learning: A Guide for Practitioners* (2001).

Designing instruction involves many interrelated activities: assessing your needs and strengths as an adult educator, developing content knowledge, learning about the learners, developing an understanding of the learning contexts, developing learning goals and objectives, developing learning activities, and developing learner evaluation. In the final chapter, reflecting on and evaluating the whole instructional design process is explored.

CHAPTER 10

Evaluating the Instructional Plan

Evaluating the instructional plan begins with the first con-
ceptualization of the plan and continues until after the plan is
completed. In essence, there are three sources of information for
evaluating the effectiveness of an instructional plan: yourself,
other experts, and the learners. Evaluation consists of reflecting
on the plan, inviting others to examine the plan, and observing
how the plan works when it is implemented. The primary tool
for evaluating the instructional plan is the instructional planning guide.

INSTRUCTIONAL PLANNING GUIDE

While developing the instructional plan, you will have conducted assessments of yourself, the content, the learners' needs,
and the learning contexts; written learning goals and objectives;
developed learning activities; and devised ways to evaluate the
learners. Bringing all these components together in a unified
plan that will result in effective learning can be facilitated by
the instructional planning guide (Figure 10.1). This guide displays the objectives, learning activities, evaluation procedures,
and other factors involved in the learning process in a manner
which shows their relationship to each other; you can use it to
sequence the learning activities and make decisions about the
whole process of instruction. The planning guide provides the
opportunity to play with the format of the instructional process
and try out variations on a theme. It is a framework which allows you to think about the interrelationships of all the pieces.

INSTRUCTIONAL PLANNING GUIDE

Title_____   Page____

Instructor_____ Date____ Time____

Goals	Objectives	Activities	Assessment	Time	Materials & Media	Facilities	Other Factors

Figure 10.1 Instructional Planning Guide

The following steps will help you complete the instructional planning guide and use it as a tool for evaluating the instructional plan.

1. Review the goals and objectives to make sure they are appropriately stated and sequenced in a logical manner, and then enter them on the instructional planning guide in the appropriate columns.

2. Determine the order of the learning activities from the sequence of goals and objectives and enter them on the instructional planning guide in the appropriate column.

3. Review the sequence of the learning activities to determine if the appropriate amount of learner involvement is present — the flow can be from low involvement to high involvement, constant high levels of learner involvement, alternate low and high levels, constant low levels, or from high to low levels of learner involvement. Check to make sure that intensive activities are not placed too closely together.

4. After the order of the learning activities has been determined, add the learner evaluation processes to the instructional planning guide. Ascertain whether the evaluation processes also flow logically. For example, is a long objective test placed early in the learning process? If so, you may want to reorder the objectives and/or the learning activities so that learners are not faced with such a difficult task early in the learning process.

5. After the relationships between goals, objectives, learning activities, and evaluation processes have been determined, the time factor should be considered. How much time will each learning activity and evaluation process take? Is this a reasonable way to allot precious classroom time?

6. Last, consider the materials and media needed for instruction, facilities needed, coordination between instructors if more than one is required, and any other factors that impact on the instructional process.

CONSULTING OTHERS
IN THE EVALUATION PROCESS

Often instructional plans are developed by teams, and evaluation of the plan is ongoing in the sense that there is a constant exchange of ideas among the instructional designers. When the plan is developed by a single person, it is best to invite others to review the instructional plan. No matter how much time you have put into developing the plan, it is still easy to overlook the obvious. You can receive valuable feedback from others who are knowledgeable about the topic, the learners, and the context. Activity 10.1, Assessing the Design of the Instructional Plan, is a series of questions which are helpful for both you and others to ask of your instructional plan.

GETTING THE LEARNERS INVOLVED

The acid test of any instructional plan, of course, is how well the learners respond to it. Learners constantly evaluate the learning process; they make their reactions known through body language, comments, attendance, attitudes, and grades. Activity 10.2, Assessing the Implementation of the Instructional Plan, may aid in recognizing and interpreting the evaluative comments of the learners.

Asking for learner feedback regarding their experience is another type of evaluation. This is usually accomplished with a short evaluation form on which learners record their reactions to the learning experience. Exhibit 10.1, Sample Workshop Evaluation Form, is an example of such a form.

FINAL NOTES

Many adult educators prefer to focus on their relationships with learners and may consider developing instructional plans to be difficult and tedious, but instructional design can be an

---

ACTIVITY 10.1
Assessing the Design of the Instructional Plan

---

1. Are the goals and objectives appropriate for the learners?

2. Are the goals and objectives appropriate for the context?

3. Do the goals and objectives adequately reflect the material to be learned?

4. Do the objectives flow from the goals?

5. Are the learning activities appropriate for the learners?

6. Are the learning activities appropriate for the goals and objectives?

7. Are the evaluation procedures appropriate for the learners?

8. Are the evaluation procedures appropriate for the goals and objectives?

9. Are the goals, objectives, learning activities, and evaluation procedures matched and sequenced in an appropriate way?

10. Are the logistics such as time, materials, media, and facilities adequately arranged?

---

exciting application of your skills and knowledge to help people learn. The central idea behind instructional design is that time spent planning learning activities pays off in a more effective and efficient learning process for both you and the learners. As in all pursuits, experience and reflection can improve future practice. Several techniques can help you acquire positive experiences that will improve the teaching and learning transaction, and ensure that current practice leads to enhanced practice in the future.

ACTIVITY 10.2
Assessing the Implementation of the Instructional Plan

---

1. Has a climate of mutual trust and respect been established in which learners feel free to comment on the learning activities and process.

2. Are the learners bored because the pace is too slow or frustrated because it is too fast?

3. Are some learners threatened by too much involvement too early? Are some learners feeling left out because there are too few opportunities for involvement?

4. Does the sequence of activities flow properly from the perspective of the learners?

5. Are learners frightened by too challenging material or restive because material is not challenging enough?

6. Are there accommodations for individual learning styles within the instructional plan?

7. Are the evaluation procedures effective in helping the learners demonstrate competence as well as in helping them learn?

8. Have the learners learned? (And if so, did they learn what was expected?)

---

1. Keep in mind that you should learn about yourself, the content, the learners, and the contexts continually. Nothing remains constant, everything is dynamic and continually changing.

2. Reflect on your experiences as a planner and as an educator of adults. Share those reflections with others whom you can trust to be honest and supportive of your efforts to improve.

EXHIBIT 10.1
Sample Workshop Evaluation Form

Please respond to the following items using the scale below. Circle the number which best describes your reactions to the workshop for each item. *Do not put your name on this form; your responses will be anonymous.* Please make any additional comments you may have on the back.

Strongly Disagree	Disagree	Not Sure	Agree	Strongly Agree
1	2	3	4	5

1. This workshop met my learning needs.   1 2 3 4 5

2. The goals of the workshop were clear to me.   1 2 3 4 5

3. The learning activities were effective for me.   1 2 3 4 5

4. The evaluation of my learning was an effective measure of my learning.   1 2 3 4 5

5. The organization of the workshop was effective.   1 2 3 4 5

6. The workshop was too long.   1 2 3 4 5

7. The workshop was too short.   1 2 3 4 5

8. The facilities were appropriate for the workshop.   1 2 3 4 5

9. The instructor was well prepared.   1 2 3 4 5

10. The instructor was in touch with the learners.   1 2 3 4 5

11. The instructor was clear and easy   1   2   3   4   5
   to understand.

12. Other comments:

Thank you for your comments!

---

3. Get feedback from as many sources as possible: other experts, learners, and yourself.

4. Use technology such as video- and/or audiotape to observe yourself teaching. It may be painful at first, but it is one of the best ways to determine how you come across to the learners.

Helping adults learn is exciting, rewarding, and challenging. Educators who want to excel at helping adults learn engage in constant self-reflection regarding their skills and knowledge as adult educators; the ability to carefully think through the learning process before learners are involved is a most important aspect of this critical reflection process. Instructional design is a tool with which adult educators etch the why, how, what, where, and when of learning into a plan that ultimately enhances the learning experience for both educator and learner.

REFERENCES

Babbie, E. R. (1973). *Survey research methods*. Belmont, CA: Wadsworth.

Bergevin, P., Morris, D., & Smith, R. M. (1963). *Adult education procedures: A handbook of tested patterns for effective participation*. Greenwich, CT: The Seabury Press.

Brookfield, S. D. (1983). Community adult education: A conceptual analysis. *Adult Education Quarterly, 33*(3), 154–160.

Brookfield, S. D. (1989). Facilitating adult learning. In S. B. Merriam & P. M. Cunningham (Eds.), *Handbook of adult and continuing education* (pp. 201–210). San Francisco: Jossey-Bass.

Brookfield, S. D. (1998). Discussion. In M. W. Galbraith (Ed.). *Adult learning methods: A guide for effective instruction* (2nd ed., pp. 169–186) Malabar, FL: Krieger.

Buros Institute of Mental Measures. (1938–2001). *The Mental Measurements Yearbook* (Vols. 1–13). Lincoln, NE: University of Nebraska Press.

Cervero, R. M., & Wilson, A. L. (1994). *Planning responsibly for adult education: A guide to negotiating power and interests*. San Francisco: Jossey-Bass.

Conti, G. J. (1990). Identifying your teaching style. In M. W. Galbraith (Ed.), *Adult learning methods: A guide for effective instruction* (pp. 79–96). Malabar, FL: Krieger.

Cranton, P. (1989). *Planning instruction for adult learners*. Toronto: Wall & Thompson.

Cross, K. P. (1981). *Adults as learners*. San Francisco: Jossey-Bass.

Darkenwald, G. G., & Merriam, S. B. (1982). *Adult education: Foundations of practice*. New York: Harper and Row.

Dean, G. J. (1993). Understanding the adult learner: An introduction. In T. Reiff (Ed.), *The Pennsylvania adult basic & literacy education handbook for program administrators, 1993 edition* (pp. 45–46). Lancaster, PA: New Educational Projects, Inc.

Dean, G. J. (2001). Why do adult educators educate adults? [On line].

130   DESIGNING INSTRUCTION FOR ADULT LEARNERS

in T. Reiff & Ellen McDevitt (Eds.). *PA ABLE Staff Handbook, 2001 Edition*. Harrisburg, PA: Pennsylvania Department of Education, Bureau of Adult Basic and Literacy Education. Available: http://www.pde.psu.edu/able/staffhbk.html

Dean, G. J., & Dowling, W. D. (1987). Community development: An adult education model. *Adult Education Quarterly, 37*(2), 78–89.

Dean, G. J., & Ferro, T. R. (1991). *AKC judges' institute: Instructional design and teaching manual*. New York: American Kennel Club.

Dean, G. J., & Kalamas, D. (1987). Human learning and the computer analogy. *Data Training, 6*(9), 44–47.

Dean, G. J., Murk, P., & Del Prete, T. (2000). *Enhancing organizational effectiveness in adult and community education*. Malabar, FL: Krieger.

Delbecq, A. L., Van de Ven, A. H., & Gustafson, D. H. (1975). *Group techniques for program planning*. Glenview IL: Scott, Foresman and Company.

Draves, W. A. (1984). *How to teach adults*. Manhattan, KS: The Learning Resources Network.

Elias, J. L., & Merriam, S. B. (1995). *Philosophical foundations of adult education* (2nd ed.). Malabar, FL: Krieger.

Gagne, R. M., & Briggs, L. J. (1979). *Principles of instructional design* (2nd ed.). Fort Worth, TX: Holt, Rinehart, and Winston.

Gagne, R. M., Briggs, L. J., & Wager, W. W. (1988). *Principles of instructional design* (3rd ed.). Fort Worth, TX: Holt, Rinehart, and Winston.

Galbraith, M. W. (1991). The adult learning transactional process. In M. W. Galbraith (Ed.), *Facilitating adult learning* (pp. 1–32). Malabar, FL: Krieger.

Galbraith, M. W. (1998). Becoming an effective teacher of adults. In M. W. Galbraith (Ed.). *Adult learning methods: A guide for effective instruction* (2nd ed., pp. 3–20). Malabar, FL: Krieger.

Galbraith, M. W., & Zelenak, B. S. (1989). The education of adult and continuing education practitioners. In S. B. Merriam & P. M. Cunningham (Eds.), *Handbook of adult and continuing education* (pp. 124–133). San Francisco: Jossey-Bass.

Galbraith, M. W., Sisco, B. R., & Gugliemino, L. M. (1997). *Administering successful programs for adults: Promoting excellence in adult, community, and continuing education*. Malabar, FL: Krieger.

Gay, L. R. (2000). *Educational research: Competencies for analysis and application*. (6th ed.). Columbus, OH: Merrill.

Gilley, J. W. (1998). Demonstration and simulation. In M. W. Galbraith (Ed.). *Adult learning methods: A guide for effective instruction* (2nd ed., pp. 233–254). Malabar, FL: Krieger.

Grabowski, S. (1976). *Training teachers of adults: models and innovative programs.* Syracuse, NY: National Association for Public Continuing and Adult Education and ERIC Clearinghouse on Career Education.

Guba, E. G., & Lincoln, Y. S. (1982). *Effective evaluation: Improving the usefulness of evaluation results through responsive and naturalistic approaches.* San Francisco: Jossey-Bass.

Kirkpatrick, D. L. (1987). Evaluation. In R. L. Craig (Ed.), *Training and development handbook* (3rd ed., pp. 301–319). New York: McGraw-Hill.

Knowles, M. S. (1980). *The modern practice of adult education: From pedagogy to andragogy.* New York: Cambridge.

Knox, A. B. (1986). *Helping adults learn: A guide to planning, implementing, and conducting programs.* San Francisco: Jossey-Bass.

Korhonen, L. J. (1998). Nominal group technique. In M. W. Galbraith (Ed.). *Adult learning methods: A guide for effective instruction* (2nd ed., pp. 219–232). Malabar, FL: Krieger.

Krueger, R. A. (1997). *Developing questions for focus groups.* Thousand Oaks, CA: Sage.

Laird, D. L. (1985). *Approaches to training and development* (2nd ed.). Reading, MA: Addison-Wesley.

Langenbach, M. (1988). *Curriculum models in adult education.* Malabar, FL: Krieger.

Lauffer, A. (1978). *Doing continuing education and staff development.* New York: McGraw-Hill.

Long, H. B. (1990, November). *Holistic evaluation.* Paper presented at the American Association for Adult and Continuing Education National Conference, Salt Lake City, UT.

Mager, R. F. (1984). *Preparing instructional objectives* (2nd ed.). Belmont, CA: Pitman Learning.

Margolis, F. H., & Bell, C. P. (1986). *Instructing for results.* San Diego, CA: University Associates, Inc. and Lakewood Publications.

Marsick, V. J. (1998). Case study. In M. W. Galbraith (Ed.). *Adult learning methods: A guide for effective instruction* (2nd ed., pp. 197–218). Malabar, FL: Krieger.

McKeachie, W. J. (1994). *Teaching tips: A guide for the beginning college teacher* (9th ed.). Lexington, MA: D. C. Heath and Company.

Merriam, S. B., & Brockett, R. G. (1997). *The profession and practice of adult education: An introduction.* San Francisco: Jossey-Bass.

Merriam, S. B., & Cafarella, R. S. (1998). *Learning in adulthood: A comprehensive guide* (2nd ed.). San Francisco: Jossey-Bass.

Merriam, S. B., & Simpson, E. L. (2000). *A guide to research for educators and trainers of adults* (2nd ed., Updated). Malabar, FL: Krieger.

Monette, M. L. (1977). The concept of educational need: An analysis of selected literature. *Adult Education, 27*(2), 116–127.

Moran, J. J. (2001). *Assessing adult learning: A guide for practitioners* (Rev. ed.). Malabar, FL: Krieger.

Murphy, K. R., & Davidshofer, C. O. (1991). *Psychological testing: Principles and applications* (2nd ed.). Englewood Cliffs, NJ: Prentice-Hall.

Schein, E. H. (1992). *Organizational culture and leadership* (2nd ed.). San Francisco: Jossey-Bass.

Schroeder, W. L. (1970). Adult education defined and described. In R. M. Smith, G. F. Aker, & J. R. Kidd (Eds.), *Handbook of Adult Education* (pp. 41–77). New York: Macmillan.

Schumin, H., & Presser, S. (1996). Questions and answers in attitude surveys. Thousand Oaks, CA: Sage.

Scott, W. R. (1981). *Organizations: Rational, national, and open systems.* Englewood Cliffs, NJ: Prentice-Hall.

Seaman, D. F. (1977). *Adult education teaching techniques* (Information Series No. 110). Columbus, OH: The ERIC Clearinghouse on Career Education and The Center for Vocational Education.

Seaman, D. F., & Fellenz, R. A. (1989). *Effective strategies for teaching adults.* Columbus, OH: Merrill.

Seels, B., & Glasgow, Z. (1990). *Exercises in instructional design.* Columbus, OH: Merrill.

Sudman, S., & Bradburn, N. M. (1987). *Asking questions: A practical guide to questionnaire design.* San Francisco: Jossey-Bass.

Tennant, M. (1988). *Psychology and adult learning.* New York: Routledge.

Tyler, R. W. (1950). *Basic principles of curriculum and instruction.* Chicago: University of Chicago Press.

Vaughn, S., Schumm, J. S., & Sinagub, J. M. (1996). *Focus group interviews in education and psychology.* Thousand Oaks, CA: Sage.

Wlodkowski, R. J. (1986). *Enhancing adult motivation to learn.* San Francisco: Jossey-Bass.

Zemke, R., & Zemke, S. (1981). 30 things we know for sure about adult learning. *Training, 18*(6), 45–52.

INDEX